On Shares

Ed Brown's Story

by *Jane Maguire*

On Shares

Ed Brown's Story

W · W · NORTON & COMPANY · INC · *NEW YORK*

First Edition

The text of this book was typeset in RCA Videocomp Times Ro-
man. Composition, printing, and binding by The Haddon Craftsmen, Inc.

Library of Congress Cataloging in Publication Data

Brown, Ed, 1908–
    On shares: Ed Brown's story.

    1. Share-cropping—Personal narratives.
2. Brown, Ed, 1908–   I. Maguire, Jane.
II. Title.
HD1478.U6B76   1975   301.44'43'0924   [B]   75–20075
ISBN 0–393–07495–1

1 2 3 4 5 6 7 8 9

To my mother, Ruth McCullough Maguire

❧ A friend, a nationally recognized civil rights leader, not southern born, has twice read this book. "I cannot identify with Ed Brown. He is too passive." True, Ed Brown is not heroic. Is Everyman? I can only speak for myself.

But Nate Shaw, protagonist of *All God's Dangers* by Theodore Rosengarten, was a hero. Other charges were brought against him, but he was really incarcerated because he joined a union. He adopted in prison the survival tactics Ed Brown and many other poor blacks and whites daily practiced outside of prison in the sharecrop system. In it they experienced life as prisoners. Together with Nate Shaw, they considered their behavior necessary for day-by-day survival.

As Ed has put it, "There was plenty of things I was asked to do and plenty of things that was said to me. But at that time there wasn't no way to right every wrong. Sometimes the smartest dodge was just to take what the whites throwed at you and go on."

There were wardens in great numbers in this prison without walls. "One time I couldn't get my old truck started nohow. Mr. Paul Thomas come along, 'I'll let you ride, Ed, 'cause I don't believe you want to get ahead of us like a heap of the niggers. Them that ain't already got somethin damn sure not goin to get nothin 'cause we're not goin to let them have it.'

"I don't want to get ahead of nobody. All I'm tryin to do is live myself and let everybody else live."

Jane Maguire

1 In cotton pickin time when we went to the field before day the frost would be white like snow. We'd make us a big fire till the frost would vanish away and we could get warm enough to work. After I started pickin, Mr. Brown didn't want me to straighten up. "Don't look up," he'd say. His motto was Keep It Goin—whatever I was at.

A farmer and a turpentine man was what he call hisself but he was mainly a possum hunter. We was livin in Wilcox County, Georgia, before the First World War, when Ma married him.

He didn't seem to like me too good for some reason. It didn't take much to tame a chile in those days. Just a little candy or a little sweet talk would have did it. But he never tried to tame me.

In later years my sister Rose reckon Mr. Brown was so hard on her and me because we the chillen of a white man. We the light-skinned ones in the family. Ma cooked for my daddy and his wife and family for a while. Whether Ma loved him or just had to let him have his way, I don't know. In them times a colored woman couldn't hardly ever say no to a white man and make it stand.

Of course that happened before Ma and Mr. Brown married. But it could have made him mad. Rose figure he did vengeance on us instead of Ma.

Once I heard a white fellow we done some work for ask my stepdaddy, "Uncle Jim, why you work these chillen so hard?"

"Well, what would you say if they was on the chain gang?"

The white fellow say, "The chain gang is a place of punishment. These chillen ain't done no crime."

One mornin the other chillen was goin to school. A colored lady say to my stepdaddy, "Hey, ain't you gonna send this boy to school?"

"No, this boy got to work."

"Well, if he was mine, he'd sure go to school."

All I fault Mr. Brown for is not sendin me to school even to learn me to read and write. He sent every one of the chillen him and Ma had. Mostly I fault Ma for not talkin up for me like she should.

Saturday evenin he'd bring candy from town and pass it around to his chillen, George Washington, Julie Mae, Samuel Wilson, and Mary, but not to me. He treated me about as bad as any white man I ever knowed. From the time I was seven or eight years old I had to do a man's work.

I never was able to pick enough cotton to satisfy him, and I never was able to beat my sister Rose pickin. When I was about ten years old I picked three hundred and eighty-four pounds in one day. She picked three hundred and ninety-four pounds that day and I think before she died she picked four hundred.

A heap of times me and Rose would get to talkin about how we was loose, happy-go-lucky, before we knowed him. Now and then we would pick up a throwed-away barrel apples had been shipped in, pull off a hoop, cut it in half, get astraddle of it, and use it for a horse. Me and another boy or me and one of my sisters.

Sometimes I ask myself what kind of a boy was I. Grown people didn't treat chillen like they do now. I wasn't dogged till after Mr. Brown married Ma. But I did what she want me to, such as sweep the yard, run errands, see at things on the stove.

Our house set in the corner of a fenced-in lot that was planted in a potato patch. The potatoes belong to the man my Ma cook for. And the house was one he built acrost the street from him to rent to the colored. He would set on his front porch and whenever he saw one of us chillen grab a potato that had cracked up out of the ground, he would come over there and fuss. When he dug the potatoes he'd give us the cut ones the plow had runned over for gatherin them. Then he'd bring two hogs to root out them we'd missed.

By one or two o'clock Ma'd bring us a pan of leftover food

from the white folks' house. Certain days of the week a man would come walkin around town with as many fish as he could tote. We made up a song:

> *Yon come the fish man*
> *You better get yo' dish pan.*

Along about August, ma would stop cookin and go to pickin cotton because there was more money in it. The first work ever I member doin was pickin cotton on the farm of her bossman, Mr. Blackburn, one of the richest men around and the normalest for payin you your money. His hands was better dressed than anyone else's and they houses was sealed up from the rain. I never heard of him or his overseer beatin up anybody, colored or white.

A bunch of us got on a wagon and went there to pick cotton. Mostly I just went with ma. But I did pick some. I reckon to have been about five years old.

That year ma and all us chillen like to perish to death from smallpox. A red flag was put on our house to give notice of quarantine. When one would get up, another would go down.

When ma got better we went to the grocery store. We didn't have no money and we was feelin very weak. The fellow runnin the store told us who had got groceries from him and had never paid. He didn't say whether he aim to give ma credit. The little ones was whinin and cryin.

"My chillen is hungry. I ain't got no time to stand here listenin to ceremony." Ma reach over and got a sack of flour.

"Wait a minute, Martha," he say. "I'm goin to give you some. But I was wantin to tell you about my trouble."

A little town is not like a city. Everybody knowed we'd been down. If we'd just been sorry and not been sick, more'n likely he wouldn't have let us have nothin.

Ma was in a weakened condition from bein so sick. She had gone to birthin chillen early and, I reckon, she was tired of takin care of us all by herself. Before me come my brother Homer. Who his father was I never knowed. Then come Rose and me.

One Saturday evenin we was in town. Ma call me to her. "Yon your daddy, Ed." I looked at the white man she point at. He was tall and wore a big Stetson hat and overalls.

I was about ten. That was the onliest time I seen him. He didn't say nothin then and he never owned up to me in no way.

After I was married, a white man named Mr. Stanley told me, "I knowed your daddy."

"Yeah? What was he like?"

All he would say was, "Well, I knowed him."

Ethyl, Willie, and Bertha was the chillen of a preacher. He was sort of a jack-leg Baptist preacher and I never knowed him to help us none.

After that Ma married Mr. Brown and we all went to live on the place of his bossman, Mr. Emory Oakes. When I wasn't pickin cotton, Mr. Brown would have me cleanin out fence jams, sawin wood, pullin fodder, knockin down cotton stocks, pullin crabgrass hay, plowin, or diggin stumps. I've dug many a stump. Ten cents apiece for any we dug up, no matter how big or how little, is what my stepdaddy would get.

Rose and me used to saw fallen logs with a cross saw. Mostly there wasn't any market for them. Mr. Brown made a man's waist-high fence all the way around our house with sawed logs. Then if anybody say, "Wood!" he'd have it.

"When he die I'm gonna put a stick of wood on his grave," Rose say.

Christmas was our big time. One Christmas Eve Ma give me twenty-five cents. I taken the quarter to Mr. Emory Oakes's store, where he sold dry goods and groceries and farmin tools, and I look and figure.

"Don't take it all in candy," Mr. Oakes say. "I got apples and oranges and raisins." He give me a peck paper sack full of them things and candy and I had ten cents left for firecrackers.

My first suit of clothes—it had short pants with three buttons on each leg—and my first pair of shoes—they was bought when I was big enough to try to plow—come from Mr. Oakes's store.

Just as good as if I done it today I member slippin on them red-lookin shoes with three smooth creases, pretty little creases. I think I *have* somethin. Around and around the house I walk and when I gets back, my feet have pulled and stretched the creases out. My parents is goin to whup me, I think, but they don't say nothin about it.

But them kind of clothes was for Sunday. When you come from church you had to put on your regular outfit, which was more than likely blousy and patched and raggedty.

Sometimes Ma would put a grown man's nice clean undershirt on me. I was small. This undershirt struck me way down. I was just runnin and playin and thought it was somethin. At that time all us chillen was goin that way. No sign of pants on.

One day I heard my stepdaddy talk about his bossman, Mr. Oakes. "He one of these slow fellows. If you want to borrow a dollar from him Saturday, you got to start askin about it Monday."

Mr. Oakes would always say, "If I go slow, as many dollars will catch me as if I go fast to catch them. I figure if I go just fast enough I'll be catchin dollars from both ways."

I wasn't like that. From my earliest days I was a minute man. Once, after we move to Mr. Oakes's place, I had a mile and a half race with a horse and I winned it.

In those days the butcher would go out in the country, buy a cow, and butcher it on the place of the man where he bought it. The butcher was a colored gentleman by the name of Mr. Ed Lane. After he butcher a cow he would put it in a one-horse covered wagon and drive back to the market in Rochelle. He wouldn't sell you none of the main beef, just the head, the tripe, the feets, or the tail, and the liver.

One time when he come by home Ma told him she didn't want nothin so he went on. He was drivin a fast red horse and I reckon he had got about two hundred yards from our house when Ma call me. "Ed, take this dime and go catch Mr. Ed Lane and get some liver." Run! I run! There was four hills between my house and the town. When I come to the top of the first hill

Mr. Lane was just goin over the top of the next one. When the horse went down the hill he gained on me. When he went up the next hill I gained on him. I'd holler, "Mr. Lane!" but he never heard me. The last hill was an extra long one. I knowed I had to overtake him at the top because once the horse was goin down the other side I wouldn't be able to catch him. I'd have to go clear to town. So I speeded. Just when he topped this last hill I throwed myself into the wagon.

"My God, boy, I don't see how you did that!"

"Ma say send her a dime's worth of liver." So he weighs up my liver on a pair of draw scales and away I goes back home.

Every time he come out my way he'd say, "Where that boy?" And he had for his subject how I caught him.

"Well, I guess he'll do," my stepdaddy would say.

So I wasn't like Mr. Emory Oakes. I knowed no dollars was searchin me out. I had to run fast after change.

Mr. Oakes was a pretty fair man but his tenant houses wasn't no account. Ours was made of logs with clay between them. Coverin the clay inside and outside the house was rived boards made with a maul and froe way back before they was a sawmill there. It was the house some pioneers built and generated in when they was amongst the first white settlers.

The first winter we was there it come a very big soakin rain and the stick and dirt chimney fell in. That chimney wasn't like it had been made of lime or mortar. It was just clay dirt between sticks. So a big rain could wash out the dirt and cause the chimney to fall.

We put dirt in a big tin tub, made a big fire in that, and stayed there all winter. Talk about smoked smutty. Before we went to town on Saturday we sure had some scrubbin to do to get clean.

Mr. Brown couldn't handle a bossman as well as it have been done. But Lord knows it was hard in them days, especially if you owed him money. Whenever my stepdaddy ask Mr. Oakes about buildin us another chimney, he would twist his long red mustaches and say, "Yeah, I'm gonna send somebody to fix it." But he never did.

Many times my stepdaddy talk about how Prince, a big red horse, would joggle along like he hardly had any life in him as long as Mr. Oakes was drivin him. "But let anyone else drive him and he'll act up."

One Sunday evening we seen Mr. Oakes comin in his rubber-tired buggy, drivin Prince at a fast clip. My stepdaddy say, "He a man ain't due to drive that fast and he a man don't do business on Sunday. Why he comin?"

Mr. Oakes driv right up to the porch. "Uncle Jim, I want you to look at this." He helt up a colored picture. "He got six legs and a snout. It's the boll weevil. He done eat up Texas and headin here."

My stepdaddy already knowed about it because our pastor had told us it was in the newspaper that the white people expectin the boll weevil, they knowed where he at and how fast he travelin to Georgia.

Mr. Oakes walk behind the well where some cotton planted and tear up one of the bolls. There was a little biddy worm with a brown head, brown on the back and gray on the stomach. That was my first boll weevil. I never seen the last of him. Mr. Oakes come back with very thin burlap bags. "I reckon you chillen can help with this. Put arsenic powder in them, tie a knot, and shake the bags over the cotton so the dust go all down in it."

My stepdaddy set us to pickin up the squares that had fell off the stalk onto the ground. "Pick 'em up, pick 'em up." He burnt the squares to keep the worms in there from hatchin. People stopped that but it was one of the first ways to fight the boll weevil. It's tirin work for a chile to walk over acres and acres dustin and pickin up. But that's what we had to do.

Even Mr. Brown knocked off from work sometimes. When he went to Rochelle in the wagon to get groceries he'd let me drive. I was crazy about his gray mule named Boy. Whilst we was south of the railroad in the white section of town I wouldn't go into the stores. Other boys would be there in the yard seein at they families' mules. I'd stay amongst them.

Some boys would tell how they mule would balk and not

work. "You can't hist an umbrella behind Boy by no means," I'd tell them. You couldn't drive him to a top buggy neither, because he was afraid of that. Every mornin I curried and brushed him from head to foot and he would stand still just as nice.

When my stepdaddy finish buyin we'd load up the wagon and cross the railroad to the colored section, and I'd hitch Boy to a post or to a chinaberry tree. My stepdaddy would stay outside to bull skate with the ladies and I'd go inside the café run by Miss Sook Smith. She was a very short, stout lady with a little finger which stuck straight out to the side. I'd turn the ice cream churn or clean fish or make ham sandwiches and she'd give me some candy or let me and her chillen lick the churn. She schooled her chillen but they would be there Saturday afternoons for me to play with.

My stepdaddy and a friend of his named Will Jones would stand in front of the café big shottin money away. Mr. Jones could dig a well a day. Sometimes somebody kiddin him would say, "Hey, Well Digger!" He was usually about half drunk when he wasn't workin.

"Yeah," he'd say, "I can dig a grave, too."

Will Jones could stack his groceries on top of his head; a sack of flour, a sack of meal, then this and that, and walk right on home with them.

He had an upright wife. She had that recommendation. I haven't heard of no one courtin her. Never. They told it for true that one time Will Jones and a friend come home drunk and begin takin off they clothes and she reach to the back of the stove for a gourd she had there, fill it with boilin water, and throwed it right at them. They run clean down the road into the white folks' cemetery.

Saturday afternoon my stepdaddy and Will Jones would race to see which one could treat every lady comin down the street to a Coca-Cola or to somethin to eat.

I think the ladies thought pretty well of my stepdaddy. And I guess he was a nice-lookin gentleman when he got dressed up.

Didn't have no stomach, and he was tall and dark-skinned and made up nice and straight and he wore a trimmed mustache. But after bein an awful hard worker he wouldn't put his money in the right thing, such as a home.

Some of the ladies wouldn't take no treat. But they was all offered. In place of courtin that many I think my stepdaddy could have bought me some overalls. He knowed my knees was out and that I didn't know hardly what a shoe was.

But he would put money in the church and do anyone a favor except his family. On cold nights he'd fix a bed of sweet potatoes in the ashes in the fireplace. He'd have some potatoes with cracklins and never ask nobody else to have any. Of course, if company come they could have all they want.

Sometimes toward evenin Saturday, if my stepdaddy wasn't ready to leave town, he'd say, "Well, Ed, you can go on home." I thought it was some big thing I could drive the mule by myself.

Monday mornin my stepdaddy would go off turpentinein. That would leave me tryin to farm. I'd have to go behind the plow he set before he lef whether it was plowin good or not.

Mr. Brown didn't have nothin to plow with but one Boy Dixie. That was the first plow to come out after they quit usin wooden ones. I liked a more modern plow, an Oliver Gruber, or a Syracuse, or a Lynch Bug. My stepdaddy drug too much in his farmin because he wouldn't set the plow deep enough to get up the cotton stalks. But sometimes it would be goin too deep.

I have had someone see me havin trouble and come acrost the field. "Boy, that plow ain't doin right. Ain't it hard to go with? See can I fix it for you." He'd set it and maybe plow a little piece with it and give it back to me. But when my stepdaddy come home he'd get mad if the settin on the plow was changed.

I got so I'd go see how the Newman boys plowed. Or I'd watch Mr. Bud Lovett, a quiet white fellow that made good syrup and never did give no trouble to nobody.

My stepdaddy would buy just a scarce little bit of fertilizer, just enough to get the crop started. When he didn't back it up with more he was out of luck.

From the start I loved farmin and loved to see things grow. Seem like my stepdaddy learnt me by what he couldn't do. And he sure learnt me a lot of things he did know, like how to hunt.

Plenty of times when I would be huntin with him, five or six men, colored and white, would shoot at the same rabbit. When my stepdaddy seed the rabbit comin he would make a big show of layin down his gun. Before the rabbit got out of reach he would pick up his gun and shoot it. The men would do the shootin and killin but they let us boys tote the game home.

When I was a chile I didn't have no gun. I just had my dogs, two or three, sometimes four or five. Us boys could hunt without guns because if a dog treed somethin it was near about ours. Whenever my dog jump a rabbit, he'd get to runnin and barkin. The dogs in the neighborhood would hear him and come join.

Saturday evenins me and the Newman boys and my brother Homer used to rabbit hunt, or fish, or dig gophers. The Newmans come from a family of fifteen chillen. My first huntin friends was amongst the boys. We used to help each other find extras to eat. In those days chillen couldn't hardly get filled up. My stepdaddy set at the head of the table, ma next to him. When you went to the table your plate was in your place with all the food you was to eat. You ate what was in front of you and did not ask for more.

Then after feedin the dogs, you was to get out and go. Once when I was takin them some scraps my stepdaddy seed me eat a bite or two. "Why you eatin that dog food, boy?" He went to the smokehouse and sliced some meat off a shoulder, fried it and some hoe cakes, and set them on the table. "You better eat that," he told me. I couldn't swallow it no how no way. So he whupped me.

Sometimes after a meal if us boys was still hungry we'd steal a piece of meat from the smokehouse. On the Emory Oakes place our smokehouse was a separate buildin that set right behind the kitchen. The door was hung so it didn't fit tight. The chillen could pull it open at the bottom sufficient for a small chile to slip through.

I start through the openin when the other chillen heard Mr. Brown approachin. They turnt the door loose and run. I got my head caught.

Dried beef wasn't the only thing we picked up. We'd go into the field and get peanuts, parch them, boil them, and eat them. Or we'd pull some roastin ears and build us a fire and lay them in the ashes. By the time the shuck would be burnt good that corn was good eatin.

Or we would steal us some chickens. We had a tin spider we kept hid in the woods. We would go there with the chickens, lard, flour, salt, and pepper hid in our clothes that would be way too big and raggedty, or patched every which way.

Aw, man, the Newmans could really call theyselves sharp. They house set facin the road. Them chillen would kill chickens back in the barn, put them in they pants, or in they bosom and just come right by they parents settin on the front porch.

We fixed a nice place at the head of a branch where a stream run off the main flow of water in the swamp. Around the edge of it there was honeysuckle vines smellin sweet even from a long way off. There was no briars to speak of and black gum and pine trees for shade. It was a nice cool place for a picnic. You could make whistles out of the reed cane if you'd a mind to. And there was a wild plum orchard and vines with scuppernong grapes.

After we cook our chickens we'd set on a big white log the bark had peeled off. There wouldn't be a piece of them chickens lef.

The Newmans' father made good crops and he sure knowed how to handle women. Two nice-lookin wives live in the same house with him. About half of Mr. Newman's chillen favor one lady in they looks—not yellow, not dark, but red, and half the other—stout and dark-skinned.

Lize, the first wife, got a cancer in her breast. So Mr. Newman had a third lady come wait on her till she died. Then his second wife got sick and she died. Whether the third lady was ever a wife while she wait on the others I don't know. I used to hear my parents say he shouldn't have two wives, not livin in the same house with him.

The Newmans was workin boys. They didn't go to school but they sure could go when they got behind a plow. All the Newman sisters was mighty fast to eat up any game we caught.

Mr. Newman was the first colored man I knowed that bought a car. In them days many white people in my section drove fine horses. The general run of colored drove the boss-man's mule. On a big farm there would be two or three one-horse wagons and two or three two-horse wagons. A crowd would get together and the bossman would give them a wagon and a mule to go somewhere. There wasn't very many cars. A doctor might have one.

Mr. Newman's car was a Maxwell with a let-back top and the nearest way I know to describe it was that it was about like a 1926 Ford and all wore out when he got it.

Everyone in the Newman family was outstandin for somethin. "Bow" Dickey Newman—his legs bowed out—knowed which trees near our settlement had hollows. When we noticed fresh scratches and hair on a slick path leadin up a large tree, we'd know an animal had been goin up and down. We'd climb that tree and nine times out of ten we'd find a possum or a coon or a squirrel in his den.

When a rabbit find a small hollow, up the inside he goes by pressin his back against one side and his feets against the other.

The very best thing to twist a rabbit out of a hollow is a bamboo stick with briars and thorns. Trim the thorns off the end you hold in your hand, stick the bamboo up the hollow, and find the rabbit. Twist the bamboo until the briars stick in his fur, then pull, pull him out.

If the tree be too tall for that, "Bow" Dickey Newman and me would get us some dry leaves, a pine top or branches, and build a fire right inside the hollow and then smother it to make smoke. The rabbit would jump out if the top of the tree had a hole in it. If it didn't he'd come out of the bottom of the trunk through the fire.

A rabbit dig him out a hole in a field to fit his body and he back right up in it. In the summertime he hop out of his bed after a rain and go after clover and other green food. Me and the younger Newmans would search this out and when the rabbits come for it the older boys would shoot them.

A cottontail will run from swamp to swamp and then turn and come back. That's why an old hunter like my stepdaddy would jump a rabbit and then stand still because he knowed the rabbit would zigzag dodgin dogs and that he'll come right back where he started from. Then my stepdaddy would shoot the rabbit without runnin after him.

In August and September we'd pick cotton all day long. When night come I'd be so tired and I'd try to slip in bed but he'd say, "Boy, get that sack and turn that dog loose."

He'd make me get up and go. But he sure learnt me to hunt. I never lacked for food.

When I think of bein a boy I always think of the one good possum dog my stepdaddy ever had. White with black spots. We called him Tide, just like Tide washin powder. My stepdaddy tied a bell around his neck and learnt him to possum hunt.

Ding ling, ding ling, ding ling. Tide wouldn't bark when he struck a trail, not until he treed the possum. We could keep up with the dog 'cause we'd hear that bell dinglingin, dinglingin. By it you'd know when he had caught the possum on the ground and was shakin it. You'd have to go because you couldn't get the dog to go back after he kilt the possum.

Or Tide would be plumb fooled by the possum playin dead, limp, like a heap of rags, not breathin. The dog goes off. You'd lose the possum if you wasn't there because after the dog leave, the possum will get up and go.

One night Tide struck a trail and run whatever it was up a blackjack oak tree. My stepdaddy would have me climb after whatever the dog had treed. I was goin up—it smelt like chamber lye up there—when somethin flew out.

Mr. Brown yell, "Boy, come on down, come on down." When I come down out of that tree he was halfway acrost a field, gone, and Tide was too. I don't know what my stepdaddy seed. I heard it and you might say I felt it.

"How come you didn't get that possum?"

But he never did answer. I wonder was it a ghost.

Then Tide treed the biggest possum ever I seen, about fifteen pounds. My stepdaddy helt up a lantern and shot him in the breast. That was the onliest time my stepdaddy ever shot one out of a tree when I was with him. I reckon he thought the possum might get away. That was some heavy tote for me home about three miles. In cotton pickin time I got so tired possum huntin at night it seem like I would sleep some walkin home. Sometimes we'd be lucky. Other times it would just be a long walk in the dark.

In the daytime you will more than likely have to pull a possum out of his bed. But at night a possum will run up a tree and just be settin there. Shakin him out was some job 'cause the possum will hang on. His hind feets have five toes lookin more like fingers than toes. One toe on the hind foot work just like a person's thumbs except it don't have no nail.

So he can use his feets like hands. He'll grab a limb and try to stick. If he go to fallin he'll catch hisself by his tail and he can hang from that. When you have him just about shook loose he'll swing back over the limb and set there, grabbin hold with his four paws.

Finally I would shake him out. My stepdaddy would be on the ground seein Tide didn't damage the possum too bad. If that happen, you would have to kill him before he got a fever or he wouldn't be fit to eat.

Most times we'd be able to keep the dog off the possum or coon enough to put him in a box. In the fall, a possum will already be fat from corn, peanuts, scuppernongs, and sweet potatoes. Catch him in the summer and he'll be poor. Then it was my job to feed him.

If a possum scared in a box he won't eat till night. Keep

them there long enough and they'll eat in the day time. But I never knowed one tame enough to turn out and he won't run away. A coon you can tame and make a pet of him and he'll stay around.

If my stepdaddy shot a coon, or a possum, or squirrel, when he got home at night we'd more than likely leave our animals in our sacks hangin up on a nail on the wall. The next mornin we'd put them in fresh water to soak.

My stepdaddy learnt me the mystery of what water can do to fresh killed meat. It takes the wild animal taste out. We would take a possum and put him in a tub of water and let him get wet to his skin. Then change the water, change the water.

A possum's meat is somewhere between pork and beef, more close to pork; a coon's meat is red and strings like beef. I never did like a skint possum. Some people skin them like a rabbit or squirrel.

Ma would rub the possum's skin with salt, red pepper and black pepper and boil him up to one and a half hours if he was a tough one. Then she would bake him just like a turkey to a light brown all over. We would put Mr. Possum on a platter and he'd be layin there good and fat and lookin real pretty with baked sweet potatoes peeled around him. My stepdaddy would be proud and I would too.

But most of the time he stayed vexed with me. None of us chillen could make it with him. One white, frosty mornin when we got to the field Homer built a fire. Here come Mr. Brown stompin it out. Homer got mad and left.

Hoein cotton was what Rose and Mr. Brown had words over. She wasn't as scared of him as I was, so she hit him over the head with a hoe.

Did I catch it! I was the onliest boy at home big enough to work. He wanted me to plow every Saturday evenin. Right after lunch he would knock off and go to town but he wouldn't take me with him.

"If he make me plow Saturday evenin I'm goin to leave home," I told Ma.

"Go ahead," she say, "and plow this time but if he make you plow next Saturday you can leave."

The next Saturday come and I had to plow but I didn't leave because I didn't know for sure I could make it by myself. And it would be hard on my mother and my sisters if I was to leave.

That evenin I heard ma prayin, "It is once more and again that your weak and humble servant have knee bent and body bowed, tryin to return thanks for the many blessins you 'stowed upon us. I know you don't come at every call. But come at the needed time.

"Lord, I want you to help me. Ed is a good boy. He has never give no trouble. . . . Teach him, Lord, guide him, strengthen him. Keep him with us. . . ."

Monday mornin my stepdaddy gets up ready to plant cotton. He was runnin the planter with the seeds in it and I was goin ahead of him puttin fertilizer down. I come with my mule to the middle of the field to pick up more guano from my sister Bertha, who was handin it out.

"Drive that mule on, boy!" my stepdaddy holler.

As hard as I could I hit the mule with the line. He was used to good treatment from me and he sure jumped and away he went. I goes to the end of the field, where my stepdaddy was standin. He peek in my distributor and seen I didn't have no fertilizer. "You call yourself puttin down guano?"

"You didn't give me no time to get none."

He come at me like he was goin to jump on me. I throwed down everythin and run.

2 I goes clear to Sibbie, Georgia, to the white man that told Mr. Brown he ought not to work us chillen so hard. After one week here come Mr. Blake. He the owner of the farm where we had moved to get a better house than the one we had lived in on Mr. Oakes' place.

Part of his trade with my stepdaddy, Mr. Blake claim, was for me to work. I was to come back to another farm of his if I couldn't work with my stepdaddy.

I went back and he set me to waitin on a white fellow that was buildin a fence. He told me to bring him a post. I start to do that and another white fellow want a post. I ask him to wait a minute. When I say that he chunk a rock at me.

But Mr. Blake see me leave. "Don't leave, Ed, stay on. I won't have you work with that fellow no more."

There was another reason I didn't like workin for Mr. Blake. His wife just naturally didn't like colored people. Most people would let the hands eat in the kitchen, but she would throw the food on an old table she had outside and make us eat there. A big bird dog would set there and if you got to your meal before he did, it was yours.

"If you're not satisfied, why don't you just tie your mule and go down through the swamp till you pass the house so won't nobody see you leave?" a white man workin there ask me. When I try that I got away.

Now my stepdaddy say I couldn't come back home. I was away from March to July. I would meet Ma in town and give her any money I made. I wanted to help her but I couldn't satisfy Mr. Brown. He had a two-horse farm and without me he could only keep one mule goin.

The cholera disease struck that year and did away with his

hogs. And his mule, his cows, and his horse Mr. Blake taken. That was to pay for what he had furnished while my stepdaddy was makin a crop. He lost out.

Mr. Brown move Ma and their chillen back to the house with the stick and dirt chimney Mr. Emory Oakes never had fixed. We knowed now he wasn't going to, so my brother Homer and Mr. Brown and me built us another one. Ma said the Lord had showed her how to look right over that chimney and to notice the mulberry tree on one side the house and the china-berry tree on the other.

Ma beg me to join the church. My stepdaddy was chairman deacon for years of the Piney Grove Baptist Church and we went there. In Sunday school I'd just set and listen because I couldn't read the cards they give the chillen with the sayins of Jesus on them.

Our pastor, George Washington Paul Hill, was a tall, dark-skinned man with a long, combed-out mustache. We called him a mighty good preacher and he had a good singin voice. In them days whatever was took up in the collection the preacher would get it all. Everybody loved Pastor Hill.

On the fourth Sunday of July he would preach a sermon called Dry Bones in the Valley. Even my brother Homer would say, "Well, I think I'll go hear Pastor Hill rattle them bones."

He would start with the toe bone and show how it connect to the foot bone and how that bone connect to the heel. And he would travel right up to a man's head. His idea was to show how good God made man. All these people God made by connectin they bones with livin flesh. They inside the church.

But they a lot of dry bones layin around in the Valley. They are the bones of sinners. God has enough power to connect them if a sinner got enough faith. Then flesh begin to crawl onto the bones. And he will be back in the church, a livin Christian.

And there was the sermon about how the bald eagle bird protect her nest. The eagle bird live high on a mountain, where she lay and hatch her little ones. But she raise them in another country. Before eagle bird leave the mountain and pull out for the far country she clean herself off of all dead feathers and she teach the little ones how to fly. She take them out on her wings and dart out from under them and when they start to fall she come back under them to keep them safe. A knowledge of the eagle bird and how she take care of her young, Pastor Hill say, would teach us how the Lord take care of his chillen.

Pastor Hill try to teach us chillen about black and white. He say Adam was made from clay. Then he ask, "Was Adam a white man, or was he a colored man, or was he a red man? You can find white clay, you can find brown clay, red clay, and you can find dark clay, you might call it black."

Comin from the church that day, Ma say, "If the white people would forget my color and I would forget slavery, we could all be Christians together."

Then there was people livin who had been in slavery. My stepdaddy's uncle was a slave and he talked like his people was good to him. He liked them and he kept pictures of his marster and young marster and the whole family in his house till it burnt up. He got a pass to go from one plantation to another and he was drivin an ox and cart and just kept goin.

Old man William Paul say he walked out of slavery into freedom. He stole a bridle and when anybody ask him, "Where you goin?"

He say, "I'm huntin mistress's horse."

A white lady come to Joe McCormack to get somethin from him to write a story and he tell her, "Mistress, you don't want me to tell you how slavery was. You just think you do."

In my day it was not quite that tough, but very early I learnt to be scared of the white man. Sometime without no cause. There was the day when I was small that I lef my sack in the field. When you pick cotton you put it in a six-foot-long draggin sack made of bed tickin. My stepdaddy bought me a brand new one. When I got down from the wagon that night at home he ask, "Where yo' sack?"

"I done forgot my sack. It in the field."

"You better go git it."

Then I'd run myself to death when I got out at night thinkin about hants. I run and walk the two miles to the field, get my sack, and start home. The moon is shinin. A man drivin a horse come along. I don't want him to see me so I jump over the fence and lay down in the field.

My motto was, when I was a boy, Don't Meet Nobody. When I seen somebody comin or heard a horse, I'd step outside the road and they'd pass on by. If what was in the field wouldn't keep you from sight it was best to go into the woods. Because nine times out of ten you'd be made to dance, or to drink some whiskey. Plenty of times I'd be tired and want a ride but I wouldn't risk one on account I didn't want to be meddled with.

But the man had got too close before I got over the fence. He stop at the place I had left the road. "Who that?" he yell. "Get up and come on out. Don't I'll shoot." I was shudderin from head to foot. I come on out. "Get in the buggy." I get in. At that time my voice was mighty fine and I didn't ever get a haircut, hardly, so my hair was awful long. "What is you, a boy or a girl?"

I was just able to whisper, "I'm a boy."

He was really a machine agent but he was in our section sellin Home Comfort wood burnin stoves. I had him scared about as bad as he scared me. "It's all right to get over the fence, but get over before the one comin see you," he say.

He carry me on home and put me out and went on. My stepdaddy give me a whuppin. I did not satisfy him by sayin how scared I was to meet the machine agent.

Other things scared me when I was a chile. The parents and the grandparents had seen so much trouble they was expectin more. They would join together to keep colored chillen clean out of the way of trouble with the white people. You was as much raised by the neighbors as by your parents. If you done somethin wrong at somebody else's house, they'd whup you for it. Your parent would say, "Thank you," and then whup you hisself.

The fireplace was for the parents. There was secret things to talk about the older ones didn't want the chillen to hear. If there was trouble and you didn't know nothin you wouldn't have nothin to hide. When company come to see the older people the chillen was not allowed in the house. Unless you was called to put wood on the fire, or get some water, you did not go in there. In wintertime you'd be back in the kitchen.

Mostly the men chewed tobacco and the women dipped snuff. At night some of the women would smoke a long clay pipe with a reed in it. If the chillen come to look, a parent or a visitor would pucker his mouth between his fingers and spit. You would get hit in the eye.

But some things they couldn't keep from you. The first trouble I member was when a colored fellow from Alabama come through our county recruitin hands. The whites in our county had recruited hands in Alabama. When the table was turnt on them, they wouldn't stand for it.

The white people caught the man recruitin, taken him out, and took his watch and everythin he had on, and they like to beat him to death. I imagine they thought he was dead when they lef him.

A colored lady heard him groanin, got some men, and they pick him up and hide him away and care for his wounds. I was small, but I knowed my parents was helpin to see after this fellow.

The first lynchin ever I knowed of I was about nine years old. One Saturday mornin this colored fellow shot the overseer on Mr. Donald Clark's place near Pine View, about fifteen miles from Rochelle.

Mr. Clark was a tall, brown-haired man that wore a number eleven shoe. The whole north end of Rochelle and most everythin in it worth anythin was his'n. He was slew footed with one foot turnt slam out on account of kickin people, some said. If you was workin turpentine for him and didn't show up for work, he'd jump right on you, white or colored, it made no difference to him.

He didn't have to go to court. He was the court. And I never knowed him to be hit back. Right or wrong, if he said anythin, that was it.

He worked lots of men. If you could make it with him, you had it made with the rest of the white people. As long as you workin with him and he done the whuppin, that was all right. But he wouldn't let nobody else bother you. For protection some would say they worked for him when they didn't.

One time a new policeman, that hadn't been in town long enough to make Mr. Clark's acquaintance, lock up one of his hands. Mr. Clark overtook the policeman in front of the hotel, kicked him around the block to the railway depot, and show him the way to Pitts, Georgia.

Finally, Mr. Clark got gangrene in that leg he been kickin people with.

But it was different when a colored fellow kilt a white man. The way I heard it, this fellow—I didn't know him—ask the overseer was he goin to pay off that day. The overseer say no and later that day he come by the fellow's house and the fellow shot him. Very quick it come out all of this was on account of the colored man's wife knockin around with the overseer.

Me and the Newman boys was playin around our house. Around and around we saw Mr. Speed Dean, the high sheriff, Mr. Clark, and some other men ridin. And we heard all this shootin. That afternoon when ma and the other ladies in our settlement that cook in town come home they told us what had happened.

When the sheriff and the posse got goin you didn't know who they was goin to kill and more than likely they didn't either. They would walk right into your house and try to make you tell whether you knowed anything or not. People would run from house to house. Many lef home and stayed hid in the woods to keep from havin anythin to do with it.

The posse caught the fellow near Pine View and brought him back near Rochelle. Mr. Clark claim the first shot because it was his overseer and his hand. We could hear the shootin from our house. They say they shot him two hundred times. I don't know if that was true. But I do know that hearin the shootin brung a funny feelin. You sort of drawed up like you was dodgin it.

Later we learnt they had this fellow go up the tree, go out on a limb, fasten his own chain, and then jump off. The shootin began just about the time he was dead from hangin. The sheriff made an old colored man in Rochelle that haul slop from the hotel take this fellow down and bury him.

It was things like this we learnt when I was young. Say your Ma want you to go somewhere for her. She would tell you what she want you to do. But before you lef she'd say, "Don't be fooling with them white boys up there; and if you see them, go the other way."

We knowed if, in spite of bein careful, we run up on a bunch of white boys and they want to pick on you, just run.

There was always the danger of comin up on a white boy wantin to pick a fight because he figure he had the ups on you. And he did. If you hit him back he'd run and tell his parents. Then here would come his father to your parents. This would scare them bad. They couldn't protect you. They would have to whup you in front of this man to keep down a lot of stirment.

Pastor Hill had been tellin the parents, "If you got a chile and you think he ought to join the church, take this chile and lead him up to the Mourners' Bench and set him there so we can pray for him."

Ma ask me to join. "Course you'll do a lot of sinnin. But it's better to belong to the Church. When the Lord Jesus come again He comin to the church. It's here to lead you the right way to go."

The night I join there was seven or eight of us that went to the Mourners' Bench when the pastor ask, "Are there any sinners in the church?" He give us the invitation to accept Christ.

The choir led:

> *"Somebody's knockin at your door.*
> *Oh, sinner, why don't you answer?*

Somebody's knockin at your door.
It must be Jesus. Can't you hear him?"

And the congregation sang:

"Don't let it be too late
to enter in the Golden Gate. "

After our pastor preach his sermon the visitin preacher pray for the sinners. He come down to the Mourners' Bench and got down on his knees amongst us. He ask the Lord to take care of us, to take us in His hands.

Then our pastor open the doors of the church and give us the invitation to join. He ask us to live, to live for the Lord:
We sang:

"I'm so glad I'm here,
I'm so glad I'm here in Jesus' name. "

We often heard from the Men's Amen Corner and from the Women's Amen Corner.

And we continued in song:

". . . Steal away home,
Steal away to Jesus. "

The visitin preacher shook the pastor's hand.

They taken the sinners on the Mourner's Bench and carry us out to a lime sink behind the church and baptize us. They ask if we was willin to be governed by the laws of the church. Yes. And that make us members.

We sang:

"I am climbin Jacob's ladder.
Do you think I'll make a soldier?
A soldier of the Cross?"

After I join the church I tell myself the Christian thing to do is to go home and help my stepdaddy. I couldn't stick for long. One evenin Ma sent me down to Kramer, Georgia, to carry my married sister a rooster. The next mornin, I walk the three miles home in time to go to the field by sunup.

About eight o'clock Ma send the younger chillen to the field totin breakfast. There was a hill between our house and the field where we was hoein. It was about seven or eight acres. That would have taken until at least straight up noon. The chillen come over the hill and the sun hit them tin pails and they was shinin.

I knowed exactly what Ma had in them tin buckets: hot biscuits juicy with butter, syrup, eggs, and bacon. I was ready to eat. When the chillen come near, my stepdaddy holler, "Carry that breakfast back to the house. We ain't gonna eat till we get this field hoed."

The cotton was about knee high, almost ready to lay by. I throwed my hoe as high as I could and got over the fence and lef. I was twelve. It was the last day I was ever a boy at home.

3

Now I was on my own.

The overseer on Mr. Joe Lynn's seventy-five horse farm, say, "Yeah, I can use you layin by the crop. Take up your ten dollars a month wages at Mr. Lynn's store."

Then I didn't know any colored man that work for straight cash wages. The only cash Mr. Lynn ever paid me was two dollars to get my marriage license.

I was to eat, the overseer say, in his kitchen. His wife was a good cook and made thin, flat biscuits, and I could really sop up syrup with them.

I was to stay in a one-room house about one hundred yards from where they live. But the bedbugs so bad I couldn't sleep. When I swept out my house I got so many I was able to scoop them up with both hands. They was in my bed so bad till I pile the bedclothes out in the yard and burnt them.

Now I didn't have nothin to sleep on, so I ask could I stay with a couple who had come from Alabama to pick cotton.

I would favor them by keepin they three little chillen while they went off to church or to parties. But I didn't want to be home too much. Them was my courtin days. I could plow all day long as hard as my mule could go, then dance all night and work the next day. Once I broke into my rest so much till I couldn't follow behind the mule. I went down in the cool woods and laid down on a log and went to sleep. When I knowed anythin the overseer was standin over me. "Hey, there! Wake up! You got to cut this out, goin around every night. You stay home and take your rest."

So for a few evenins I had to wait till the lights went off in his house before I went out.

For a while I went to John Major's house. He try to learn

me to read and write but it didn't work too good. He was sort of an educated fellow and right off he want me to speak proper. I couldn't do that.

Most of the time I didn't have any way to get around unless I walked. But I was good at that. I walked to church and to meetins of the Young Men's Progressive Club, which was to give courage so you wouldn't be 'shamed to say things before anybody else.

When we come together the preacher would give you a topic, such as which was the most value a horse or a mule, or a cat or a dog. You'd have to the next meetin to study about that. You'd have two sides and judges to tell which would win. We wanted to know who could show the most points and argue the best case. I liked it and to myself I used to pretend I was really a lawyer.

The old folks would set there listenin to us. And then you'd walk your girl home. In them days you walked with a girl in front of her parents, not behind them. That was what I wanted, a girl.

A certain girl was to be at the revival at Kramer, Georgia. Mr. Lynn said I could borrow his brown bayish horse. That horse had a real good single foot and after we crossed over the railroad we really went. A skunk come across the road and when the horse runned over it, the skunk let go his musk and spread it with his tail.

That is a strong odor. I've had dogs that could kill a pole cat. But they're no more good for huntin that night. That smell makes them sick. It'll make anyone sick.

Man, I had me a cologne from there to the church. One step through the door and folks helt they noses, open they mouths, and fan theyselves hard. That was a known scent. Who had brung it? The girl I had gone to court throwed back her head and laughed. I got up and went on out.

Next I favored Mel Vinney. Her mother wanted her to marry Whittey Blackshear. He was a rich boy. Not rich exactly,

I guess, but his father rented land to farm with and owned his own mules.

One day Whittey and me was setting on Mel's porch. Whittey comes out with his pocketknife and say, "You see this? This means blood."

I knowed he was toting a knife. My brother Homer had give me his pistol. I brung it out, "You see this? This means death."

Mel's mother comes flyin. "Nobody better come back here to see Mel except Whittey Blackshear."

"Well, you got her," I told Whittey and got up and lef.

But she didn't want him. About a week after that I seen Mel. "You ain't come back to see me."

"No, your ma don't want me in the family."

"You ain't courtin my ma. You courtin me."

The first sex I ever had was with a lady tryin to make some money to get her husband out of jail. She begged me to do it.

If the jail full and help got scarce, landowners would get hands out of jail Monday mornin and work them gatherin tobacco or choppin cotton or whatever there was to be done. They liked that better than stayin in jail. They'd make a little money, too. Saturday evenin the landlord would take them back to jail.

This lady—I don't know her name—was in jail and so was her husband. Why she there I don't know. He had stole some cotton. Me and her was choppin cotton on Mr. Sam Gibb's place. His boy, about nine years old, was workin there with us. When the idea come to me to take up this lady's offer I knowed I had to get rid of junior.

"I want me a drink of water," I tell him, just like I was so thirsty I was about to perish to death. I knowed he'd be gone awhile if I had him to tote water because we was workin on the back side of the field. He was a fat, slow fellow and it was near about half a mile there and back to the well behind his daddy's house.

We done it right in the field. I promise her money but before I got any she had got away from there.

One good thing come of workin for Mr. Lynn. Willie Mae Sparrow—fourteen years old—was choppin cotton there. I met her at the church and ask her about walkin home. She had been married, she told me, for twelve months to a fellow from Alabama. Whether her husband already had a wife at home I don't know. But I suspicion that's what cause him to slip off from Wilcox County when business got sort of tight.

Some said Willie Mae wasn't the prettiest girl in our settlement but I never did see no other as pretty to me. I thought a lot of her. I commenced to carry her to various churches and to root workers. One Saturday evenin I told the overseer, "I want the mule and buggy to take a girl to town."

"Sure enough? Well, I reckon I'll have to let you have it."

I slicked that mule down, curried him, and put a red tossel on his bridle to make him look pretty. Away we went.

The minute we walk in the house of the lady root worker in Hawkinsville she tell us, "You come to see is you suited for marryin. You ain't cousins, is you? Don't marry too deep in the family if you don't want deformed chillen." She give us a cup of tea. "This is red sassafat. It sure ain't white sassafat 'cause that will cause you to go blind. You all ain't goin to stay together."

"If we part we ain't goin to be the first ones," I say.

When we married in 1920, Willie Mae was fourteen and had some education. I was close to turnin sixteen.

"Well, I hope you'll stay together," the preacher's wife told us. "But I ain't expectin it. You married too young."

"You need courage?" Willie Mae's ma ask me. "Put a coon root in some whiskey and let it set, then pour off a little of the whiskey and drink it just before you go to bed."

We walked home.

Willie Mae was one to beautify a place. Our house, just a shell of a house not sealed in any way—no plaster, no ceilin—had a chimney goin up from a fireplace openin on to two rooms, so some called it a stacked chimney double pen house. In place of glass windows it had shutters of upright boards that swung out on hinges like a gate. Flour sacks with the writin bleached off make nice curtains. Soon she had them up.

In the house there was a number seven stove—that's a small cast iron stove with four eyes—a bedstead and a table for eatin. Ma give me a quilt, a pair of pillow cases, two sheets, and told me to take my three chickens she had been keepin for me. My wife's mother give her a mattress, a dresser with a mirror, and a crippled white hen.

We use nail kegs for chairs and we had an iron kettle, a black pot, and a fryin pan.

And for forty years, before we parted, we lived together man and wife.

Every fourth of July Mr. Lynn would give a barbecue for everybody that worked on his farms. I don't care how many chillen you had, all of them was considered Mr. Lynn's hands.

What land he didn't own in the settlement he rented. He was the only man I ever knowed with five gins settin in a line. And there was a cypress log hollowed out for a water trough on one of his farms that thirty mules could drink from at one time.

Workin for a small man you had to feed your mule, and pump water for him at the trough. At Mr. Lynn's you just turnt over your mule to the lot man. He didn't do nothin but see after the barn and the stock.

On a big farm nearly always there's an outstandin man like a preacher or some big deacon. Mr. Lynn would have the barbecue at that man's house. Every July third two or three cows, two or three hogs, and some goats was butchered. Men worked all night cookin. And they'd make Brunswick stew out of the heads and the feets.

July fourth, the women would come with cake, light bread, lemonade, ice tea, potato salad, potato pie, and other pies.

About nine or ten o'clock Mr. and Mrs. Lynn—both of them big and stout—would come and get what they want to carry back to town. Or Mrs. Lynn might say, "I want you to fix us a table." We'd put a big table with some of everythin on it off in the shade and them and they daughters, all big and fat, would fill up.

Then Mr. Lynn would turn everythin over to the hands. He would tell the man havin the barbecue at his house, "I don't care about you all playin cards or shootin a little crap, but don't hurt anyone."

There was always stump liquor. I don't care if a party be to the church, stump would be there. Money was so scarce you couldn't buy much of it. If you got half a pint it wouldn't be enough for you and a friend to get drunk.

There would be a ball game and people would stay until the food and whiskey was gone.

Nobody ever figured out Mr. Lynn's bookkeepin or how he did things. If it was a good year, he'd try to help his hands. If it was a bad year, he'd be head over heels in debt and then his hands didn't get nothin. You could make a good crop and still be lef in a hole. A lot depend, Mr. Lynn said, on what he got out of it.

I wanted somethin for Christmas for my wife. So December twenty-fourth I goes to Mr. Lynn's commissary and set around till way after dark.

Then you never seed nobody with money hardly. If you had plenty to eat and a good pair of overalls to go to town, you was doin pretty good. Mr. Lynn claim I had took up sixteen dollars more than he owe me at the store. I don't know how he figured that but you couldn't argue.

Finally I ask him would he let me have some apples and oranges.

"No," he say, "I ain't puttin out nothin for Christmas."

"Well, would you let me have a piece of backbone?"

"Yeah, I'll give you that."

So I got the butt end of a hog's backbone, about four pounds. But I was right dissatisfied. When I got home my wife's sister and her husband, Tommy Woods, from over at Cochran tell us how good things was there.

The man he work for want a hand. He had sent Tommy for one. They stayed around a day or two eatin up the backbone.

You couldn't just walk off if you owe a fellow. And if you didn't owe him and he want you to stay he'd get you in some sort of flaw, some sort of debt so that the new man you work for will have to pay the old employer to get you.

But me and my wife decide to go with her sister and Tommy Woods to Cochran. We lef Mr. Lynn's soon as it got dark enough so that wouldn't nobody see us. We was running away.

4 It was my first time out of Wilcox County walkin or ridin. We was wearin everything we had except what was in a round egg basket: a sheet and a pieced quilt top not quilted. Tommy Woods had thirty cents and a 32 Smith and Wesson pistol.

A bad storm come up with plenty of wind. We spreaded the quilt top on the floor in an old empty house and laid on that and took the sheet to cover the four of us. Way before day we got away from there because we didn't want the people ownin the deserted house to know we was there.

It was cold and damp from rain and I was about numb. When the sun come up red we was on highway 129. A fellow come along with a wagon and carry us right up to the red light in Hawkinsville. Mostly I want to hide from the big town. I had a pair of overalls and the cheapest quality shirt you could get at Mr. Lynn's store. A friend of Tommy's set us right up to his fireplace while Tommy pawned the gun and got a man with a T Model to carry us the ten miles from Hawkinsville to Cochran.

Mr. Jim McHenry—he was red faced and had a big stomach —hired me. Ten dollars a month, sixteen pounds of home-cured hog meat, and a peck of meal was what he would pay, he told me and my wife. And we could have all the corn we wanted to shuck and eat. We had to see at some chickens and we couldn't kill none of them but we could have the eggs.

My wife washed for Mrs. McHenry. At that day and time some of the white people would have white muslin covers to put on the backs of straight back chairs in the summertime. That was to make things look cool, they claim. My wife had washed Mrs. McHenry's napkins and chair covers and done them up.

We give a party. We put the napkins on the table and the covers on our three straight chairs. To my wife's mind things was lookin very pretty. The party had got started good when in pops Mr. McHenry and his son. Mr. McHenry stood there in the doorway and smiled. "You all are really havin a big time, aren't you?"

I can't say I was lookin for him. After a minute or two the McHenrys left. My wife say, "I could have went through the ground."

They never knowed, I don't think, about the linens we used because they didn't ever mention it. My wife washed them and done them back up.

One evenin a big hailstorm come up. I took the mule to the barn but I didn't feed him. When I got to the house I went to sleep. I was aimin to feed the mule later but when I woke up it was way in the night.

When Mr. McHenry start cussin Tommy because he hitch one mule to a two-horse plow, Tommy told him about me not feedin the mule.

I was diggin up a stump to keep the buggy wheel from hittin it. Mr. McHenry come up to me real close and ask, "Ed, did you feed the mule last night?"

"No, sir." I tell him how it come up a hailstorm.

"If hail come up big enough to bust your brains out, you better feed my mule."

Me and my wife and Tommy Woods and his wife talk about how we was goin to run away again.

Time we decide to go my wife cut up the one sheet Mr. McHenry had furnished us and make herself three underskirts. She write ma and tell her we want to leave. Ma come with Mr. Jake Fish, the new overseer on Mr. Joe Lynn's place, where she was livin. My brother Homer is layin at the point of death and if I want to see the last of him I have to come and that is the reason they come at me, she told Mr. McHenry.

He owed me nine dollars. Me and my wife had lived stingy and had only taken up one dollar of my wages at the store. I asked for my money but Mr. McHenry suspicion I am tryin to leave. "You sure you got a brother? You know you been wantin to leave for the longest. I'm goin to pay you when you come back. You know I think a lot of you."

But he knowed I wasn't comin back. Many years later when the government went to helpin the poor man, they passed a law the employer had to pay wages if the tenant work so much as a day.

My wife put the three underskirts on and we packed the little we wasn't wearin and lef.

On the way back, somewhere after we pass Cochran, Mr. Fish stop and take his pistol out of the tool box on the runnin board of the car and goes to tinkerin with it. "Ain't nothin wrong with your brother. I just told that to get you away from Mr. McHenry."

Mr. Fish driv up in Mr. Lynn's yard and there was the bossman standin in the barn. He had them same heavy eyebrows but he had took on weight. Mr. Lynn tell me he is mighty curious as to why I lef.

"Because you didn't give me no Christmas," I say.

"Well, you didn't ask me for none. Next time ask me and I'll put out some."

Every Christmas after that, if I ask him, he'd let me have half a backbone or a few oranges or three or four apples or a little candy.

But I was on wages and I didn't like that.

Wages not a good thing to work for if you want any pleasures. On shares if you're a good farmer you try to be through layin by corn, cotton, and peanuts by July fourth. Then you set around and eat out the garden and go to church. In the summertime you fish a heap.

Revivals start in July and run on till fall. We'd have a visitin pastor come and run our meetin for us. There would be five days and five nights of preachin and prayin. Each day after the eleven o'clock sermon, the pastor would go to another brother or sister's house for a big lunch.

The man entertainin the visitin pastor would invite the regular preacher and the deacon and his wife and a friend or two. The ladies would argue back and forth about what to eat. To my wife's mind nothin ever tallied up as good as fried chicken. Then you might have an old ham, corn bread, biscuits, preserves and jelly, butter beans, turnip greens, and pie and cake. When it was put on the table the man of the house would say, "Friends, fall in here and let's eat."

But you couldn't join in the fun if you was on wages and your time belong to the bossman. After you laid by the crop he'd have you cuttin logs at the sawmill, doin road work, and cuttin ditches. On rainy days you'd be in the crib shuckin corn or haulin black manure or compost, or cleanin out fence corners.

After a while I want to work on shares. I goes to Mr. Bill Jackson, Mr. Addison's overseer, and say, "I hear you have a farm to let on shares."

"Yeah, I got one." But he didn't show it to me.

When he show me a mule I knowed it was the best to say, "Now is this the mule I'm goin to work for the year round?"

"Yeah, that's your mule. If you come work for wages a while I reckon I'll have a farm for you in January. I'd like you to go to the Furgin Company and trade. It would help me." The folks at the store told Mr. Jackson I hadn't come. "How come you ain't tradin at Furgin's?" he ask.

"The only pair of shoes they got to fit me cost twelve dollars."

"Well, I don't have no more work and I can't pay you now," he say.

I fished and rabbit hunted to keep eatin till the first of January and I find me some work here and there by the day.

Then, on a farm in south Georgia, January was mostly clean-up month. You cut stalks and pick up litter you don't want to plow under. Unless it's Sunday everyone hired on shares meet the overseer at the barn by sunup January 1.

When I got there Mr. Jackson was sayin to one tenant, "You take this mule," and to my brother-in-law, "you take that one." He didn't give me my mule.

"Where my farm?"

"Wait a minute," he say. "Me and you will get together directly." Then he give everybody else furnish money, the first since last June. "Let's me and you walk up the road apiece," he say. We start walkin. "I had to let my brother-in-law have the farm I been promisin you."

Soon after actin so slippery with me, the Klan give Mr. Jackson a whippin that laid him up for days. He was the first white man I knowed to be tore up by the Klan. He frolicked a lot with the ladies. The hands that was workin for him at the time told me he received warnin but he didn't heed it. I wasn't too sorry to hear about his trouble.

My wife was comin due with a baby. I had to hustle. In 1923, I hired out to make my first crop on shares with a man that, as the Lord would have it, had the same name as me. People took to callin him the white Ed Brown and me the colored. I guess you might say he was nice. But he just didn't have nothin. He was poor.

A poor man's word don't go as far as a rich man's word. The fifth of August my wife was in labor. "Mr. Brown," I ask, "could I have some money to get a doctor?"

"I ain't got a bit of money but you can try to get a doctor on my word I'll pay."

I made several trips to town. "Mr. Brown already owes me money," Dr. Hunter told me. "I won't be able to come."

I left his office and got me a granny woman. She come Saturday noon and give my wife tea made from roots. About three o'clock Sunday evenin my wife's stepdaddy call me out my house. "That baby ain't born yet?"

"Not yet."

"Here, take this ten dollars and go to town and get you a doctor."

This time I got a doctor by the name of Dr. Durham. "I've

been noticin you walkin around and around here." We driv up to my house in his car, "What do you want, a boy or a bushy-headed gal?"

"I'd rather have a boy."

Soon after he come he say, "You're goin to have to settle for a girl."

The granny woman and the ladies that was there wash the baby and put her in bed with my wife.

That day was her birthday. She was sixteen years old.

Lottie we named the baby. Two little white girls we knowed come and knelt down by the bed. One of them told me, "Oh, Ed, this is the prettiest baby. I believe this is a blue-eyed baby."

"Oh, no!" I say, "that just the baby look." And it was.

Mr. Brown sub-rented a six-horse farm from Mr. Emory Oakes. Bein a poor man, he didn't poison the cotton. It rain most all that year and what with no poison and not much sunshine the boll weevils just cleaned us out. I made just one bale of cotton—the sorriest crop I ever made farmin. Corn was so cheap I couldn't begin to pay my debts with it.

Mr. Brown got clean wiped out. "Well, Ed, you don't owe me nothin and I don't owe you nothin." He cut off my furnish money and me and my wife didn't have nothin to eat except what was in the garden and some chickens she raised.

But we was lucky. Some people wouldn't let you keep anythin that might eat any part of the crop that come up around your yard. With other folks like Mr. Brown you could raise as many as you liked and have as fine a garden as you could make.

Now Mr. Brown and me had to leave. "Ed, I ain't got no money to pay you, but if you'll help me move, come down home Thanksgivin and I'll give you a big dinner."

Course the Browns was renters and didn't have no land and they wasn't above eating rabbits 'cause me and Mr. Brown had hunted lots of them together. I help them pack two wagons full of household stuff and take it about six miles to the next farm they was movin to. Then we unpack and set everythin in place. It was a hard day's work.

Thanksgivin I goes to their house. I stood around and ask them was they enjoyin the holiday. Mrs. Brown give me a piece of coconut cake that was sliced so thin you could near about see through it. When I left she said, "Ed, I sure hope you had a good Thanksgivin."

5 Nineteen twenty-five was one of the best years for cotton. The gins went by steam and they would run day and night. I have been to the gin when there were so many wagonloads of cotton that it would take three days to get a bale ginned.

That year most of my friends come out of debt and some cleared about seventy-five dollars, or one hundred dollars, or two hundred, according to how big a family a man had. Some bought cars.

After Mr. Brown lost out I went to work for wages.

Then every time you come up in the world you got a better mattress. On wages you'd have a mattress made of wheat straw or oak straw or crab grass. On shares a man that was looking out for hisself could keep back or steal, you might call it, some of the cotton he was supposed to take to the gin.

On a mattress made of unginned cotton, the trouble was, unless the tickin is mighty thick, you can feel the seeds. On standin rent the whole crop belong to you and you could have a mattress of ginned cotton. That's what my wife wanted.

The landowners was beggin hands to come and work. Mr. Emory Oakes give me a good little farm on shares a mile east of Rochelle. We was off to ourselves with no bossman on the place. So we got a nice mattress of unginned cotton. And that was where I made my first real money.

Me and my wife made out a plan to fool Mr. Oakes and it worked. I picked nine bales of cotton. Then I went to him and ask for our settlement. He figured that this year I had come out of debt and made three dollars.

Two weeks later I goes back, "I got another bale."

"Why didn't you tell me this to start with?"

"I thought I had done picked it all but that cotton just kept on openin up."

Cotton was bringin about twenty-two cents a pound. "Well, I reckon I'll have to pay you then."

One week later I take yet another bale to Mr. Oakes. "Look a here," he say, "I ain't looked at the meat book for things you got at the smokehouse. How much you owe me?" He was a man to say, "Don't buy any meat or syrup in town. You can get it from my smokehouse."

I ain't been down to the smokehouse to get no meat."

He thought a while. "Look like we made us some more money." But he didn't seem exactly happy. I think maybe if I had taken the eleven bales to begin with I might not have made any more than when I took nine. Instead of the three dollars Mr. Oakes first figure he owe me, I made one hundred and fifty dollars.

For a man without no education I was plenty schemy.

The reason I not to go to Mr. Oakes's smokehouse was I went on rabbits, possum, fish, or whatever I could find that didn't cost money. There was about as many rabbits inside the town line as in the country. My meat market was the part of the river swamp next to the jail on the east side of town.

I kept me some good dogs and whenever we needed food I went after it. If you like to hunt there's always the excitement of catchin somethin you like to eat.

If you ain't got money for gunpowder but you got a good dog you can still hunt. Every time I walk out of my house quite natural my dogs was ready to go. One evenin when I went to get some kindlin I notice four little fox squirrels playin up a pine tree. I taken me a piece of wood and chunk them out one by one. The dogs picked them up for me.

A three-legged dog was one of the best I to have. One hind leg was chopped off just above the knee. He would hop along but when he struck a trail he could go pretty fast.

A black shepherd with a white ring around the neck was another smart animal. He was give to me by a wood rider—he the turpentine hands' bossman that ride over the woods to see if all the boxes is chipped and if each tree has a cup on it for the gum.

He wanted to leave the dog because I was on a farm and could feed him.

"What's he good for?" I ask.

"Nothin, 'cept to play with the chillen."

He strayed back to town. The wood rider brought him back. I was down by the branch strippin cane gettin ready to cook up my syrup. "Keep him out here," he say. "I ain't got nothin to feed him."

I was tired of argument. After lunch I carried him back to the cane patch. He start running rabbits. Right then I took a likin to him.

My wife soon learnt he could drive up the stock. The first time I knowed him to do it we was settin on the porch havin a big time with Chester Lemon. "Will you excuse me? I got to go get the cows and milk them."

"Just send Shep after them," my wife say.

"Dis I gotta see," say Chester Lemon.

She call, "Shep, go get the cows." Over the fence he went and around that field and get them cows and bring them to the house.

That made Shep a member of the family. You could tell him, "Go yonder and get them cows, or them hogs, or them mules." And he could do it just as good as any chile. He knew my cows from other peoples. If a strange cow got on my place, he'd be after it.

Once I had a dog to take up with me that didn't look no good. He'd go to the field and walk around and around with me while I plowed. He was a setter. I hadn't thought much about him. One day I pull my jacket off and put it down. This dog laid down by it. A rain come up and I just taken my mule and went to the house.

Two or three days later after my field had dried off I goes back, hitches my mule, and plow around to the place where I left my jacket. And there was that dog layin on it. Well, I say to myself, this must be some fine dog. What he calls hisself doing is takin care of my jacket. He had about perished to death.

This dog wasn't much on rabbits but he was a good bird dog and I thought the world and all of him.

Colored and white and dogs and the animals we was after would all be in huntin together. We'd sometimes kill twenty-five or thirty rabbits and then colored and white, we'd go to a bubblin spring, where we'd skin and dress our rabbits and boil them in wash pots until the meat would fall off the bone. Then we would roll the meat into little round balls like hamburgers, add salt and pepper, roll it in a little flour, and fry it. And we would make hushpuppies. You talk about eat, that's good eatin.

The white folks would most likely play cards and drink stump liquor. And they'd pour us colored some in a tobacco can. Go out in the woods with one white man and you can get along like brothers. But let another white fellow come along and seem like both of them want the other to think he know how to treat a nigger.

Once some of us half croppers was huntin rabbits with Mr. Oakes's overseer, Mr. Archie Fergusson, and some other white fellows. A rain come up and we all went to a barn and set under the shelter. A colored man, Lawse Johnson, ask Mr. Fergusson for a cigarette. Lawse done just like he had been doin when Mr. Fergusson give him cigarettes. He pour him out some tobacco onto the cigarette leaf and helt that in his left hand. And to close up the tobacco bag he put one string in his mouth and pull the bag shut with his right hand. It was somethin that just come natural.

When he done that Mr. Fergusson hop up and holler, "Don't you put my tobacco strings in your mouth."

Lawse said, "Aw, I'll bite 'em off," just like he was makin a joke.

The trouble was Mr. Fergusson didn't want the other white

fellows to think he wasn't clean. Lawse Johnson was clean and Mr. Fergusson knowed it, but he was afraid of what our boss-man, Mr. Oakes, would say and of what the other white folks would think.

I liked Mr. Oakes and he liked me. But they was a white fellow named Horace Martin live right back of me that stay drunk all the time. The only way he could get to highway 280 was to go through Mr. Oakes's property right by my house. Two or three times a week he'd lay down on my porch till he got sober enough to go home.

Me and my wife would come home and find him there and just go on in the house. Mr. Martin never did come inside.

One evenin a friend of mine named Major come and seen Mr. Martin layin on the porch. "What he doin there?"

"He be drunk and I just let him lay there. He don't bother me and I don't bother him."

"Well, damn if I'd let him lay on my porch."

Mr. Martin wasn't as drunk as he was makin out to be. He heard everythin Major say. The next time he got drunk he went over to Major's and laid on *his* steps.

Major say, "Look a here. You gotta get away from here. You belong over at your house." Mr. Martin drug on up, "I'll go, I'll go." And he went.

Another day when Major was there Mr. Martin come back to my house. He ask, "Major, don't you want a drink of liquor? Go to yonder telegram pole and get you a quart."

Major went and looked. We was standin there watchin him and Mr. Martin say, "Look at that nigger puttin my liquor in his pocket."

"Well, you sent him at it. Let's go and see is he got it."

When we got there Major say, "I don't see no liquor here."

"I seed you put it in your pocket," Mr. Martin say.

"No, I didn't," Major say. "If you don't believe me you can search me."

That was exactly what Mr. Martin want to hear. He

searched Major not for liquor but for a gun. When Major didn't have one, the fun began. Mr. Martin took out a 38 Colt, and throwed it on him.

"Don't shoot him! Don't shoot him!" I say. "We'll find the liquor."

Me and Major was like two bird dogs let out of a car. When we got a good little piece off I say, "This is as good a chance as we're goin to get to run." We lit out down the road to where it went in two ways, one to Major's house and one to mine.

When we separate, Mr. Martin start shootin at Major. He was goin so fast the long black overcoat he had on was flyin back behind him in the air. It was so flat you could have shot marbles on it.

I ran to my house and got my wife and we took to the woods. When we went home the window at the back of the house had been broke into. Mr. Martin seen me later, "Ed, I tore your window open to tell you I'm not goin to bother you. I was after Major. You know how bad he treated me when I lay down on his steps."

"Yes, sir."

I go to Mr. Emory Oakes and tell him I'm scared and I'm leavin there.

Mr. Oakes say, "Well, you colored people won't stand up for yourselves none. I hate to see you leave but I know you don't want to stay out there and get hurt."

6 Ever since his overseer promise me a farm and then give it to his brother-in-law, I had wanted to work for Mr. Addison. The overseer say this time he ain't foolin, I can have a farm. But before I could move he got turnt out account of drinkin.

So I goes to Mr. Addison and he give me a one-horse farm on shares, and time he done that Mrs. Addison sent for me.

"Ed, I want to tell you a story. Once there was a man. A fellow come to him and say, 'I want you to kill your brother-in-law.'

"The man got mad. 'I wouldn't kill my brother-in-law for nothin in this world.'

" 'Well,' say the fellow, 'what about drinkin a quart of liquor?'

" 'I'll drink all the liquor you can get me.'

"The man drank the liquor and killed his brother-in-law. Now, Ed, don't drink."

After that I never went around Mr. and Mrs. Addison or her sister, Miss Berk, when I had took a drink. But they was the best people I ever worked for. You could put your foot on anythin any of them said and stand firm.

When it come time to take our cotton to the gin, Mr. Addison would say, "You made the crop, you sell it and bring me the papers." Us half croppers would know what we made.

At the gin it was a very pretty sight to see the seed rainin down into a trough and the lint just a flyin back the other way into a pipe. We'd talk about how we was goin to pay our debts with the lint and eat the seeds.

Cotton is a crop I like to work and it look beautiful when you got a nice field of it. I don't care if you seed it the day before, it'll be different. First the square, then a white bloom that turn almost purple, and die and shed off. Then you get a little boll there.

There's more work in cotton than any crop I ever tended. But I never did want to farm without it and I always paid my debts with it pretty good. Plenty of times I'd hear, "Ed, I wisht I had you on my place. How do you make such a good crop? I want some of your seeds."

"My seeds the same as everybody else's." But I had some good land. That make a big difference.

Your two worstest enemies if you was a sharecropper was the boll weevil and the landlord. Many a time the sharecropper's family would live stingy and do all the work in the crop they-selves. Then the boss would tell the tenant he wasn't goin to get nothin else. "You done eat up your half."

After the crop is laid by, when you have nothin to do but gather your crop, some men will make you leave. I've been taken for every dime in my part of the crop and wiped out with nothin. And it could be a boss who calls hisself the best man in the world. Maybe he don't go all the time but he holdin up the church for his wife.

You got to know how to make good trades with your boss-man or he'll wipe you out. Ten dollars a month wages. Then some people started payin fifteen. When Mr. Addison say, "I'll pay you ten," I had to speak up.

"No, sir, Mr. So and So over there is payin fifteen. I got to make fifteen."

"Well, I reckon I'll give you fifteen."

Beginnin in January I'd be on my feet by sunup and me and my mule would be goin day after day until the land was broke up and turned.

At first Mr. Addison say, "How is *your* crop, and how is you gettin along turnin *your* land? Take care of the mules. Don't rush because I want them to last."

Any place I ever farmed in Wilcox County we was in har-mony farmin. We helped each other. I didn't have a section harrow but some big man nearby would have it and I could borrow it for givin him some of my time. Now I'd get my one-horse farmer friend, white or colored, livin nearby. I'd borrow his mule so I could use his and mine behind the harrow to tear up clods and get my land level and smooth. He would get my mule to do the same thing on his place.

In February to my mind it was usually too cold to fish. But we went on breakin and turnin land and pulverizin it. And we went rabbit and coon and possum huntin.

I'm goin regular to the boss about once a month for furnish money. "Ed, when you goin to start plantin your crop?"

"I'm waitin till the moon quarter, about the fifteenth of March."

In March with a four-inch scooter on a hayman stock I'd streak off my rows to plant cotton. About the fifteenth I'd put in some soft corn to give me early feed for my hogs and cows. Then I'd have almost two weeks in March and all of April to plant cotton.

Now I'd give one of my good neighbors his rathers whether he want to run the fertilizer distributor or the cotton planter. When we got my cotton planted, I'd go to his house to help him.

Along about April the bossman would say, "Ed, is *your* cotton gettin ready to chop?"

"I always chop when it get about three leaves on it. That way I can tell what's goin to die and what ain't."

In the first years I farmed I'd get a crowd of chillen and I'd give each chile a half-gallon bucket and they'd strew the soda by hand alongside the cotton. I'm comin along behind them with my mule and cultivator coverin the soda with dirt. The sun heat the dirt. The rain melt the soda and it go to the cotton and turn it green.

If I have good weather the cotton will come right up, about a half a leg high. I don't plow deep the first time I cultivate it in May. I gotta go light because it ain't got such a good holt. It look so pretty pointin toward the sunshine in the east. It go with the sun. Over like that. Just the top of it.

Soda it, back it up plowin, soda it again. Now it got about

four, five, or six leaves on it and it about six inches high or seven, gettin up to where I can plow deep and loosen up the ground good around my crop.

All the time I got to be thinkin what to do. One time the last of May there was a big hailstorm. It beat the corn and the cotton level with the ground. Most of the people decided to plant over. I was ahead of the rest of them with early cotton. When I seen some little buds comin out on the stalks I took a chance and did not plant again. I picked eleven bales of cotton behind one mule and plowed three under for the government.

Mr. Addison ain't come out yet. He still settin to the office leavin it in my hands.

"Well, it look good," I tell him. "It's loaded down with squares and I seen a bloom this week." In about a month he ask again. I look down around the bottom. "That cotton sure bollin up." I got to tell him it's pretty good 'cause I've got to get somethin to eat out of it. I plow my cotton for the last time. It's laid by till time to pick. Furnish money ends.

Now the boss ask, "Is *our* cotton doin pretty good?"

I tell him I wants somethin to eat.

"Ed, it takes right smart to make a crop. I ain't able to furnish you nothin else. I borrowed money everywhere I could and I've spent it all tryin to get this crop up to where it's at. Don't you believe that?"

"Yeah, I believe it. Still I got to eat, you know."

In July when the furnish money has give out my meat is about give out too. But I know he tellin the truth. He in a tight too.

"You got a garden? We got to eat out of the field," he say. Maybe I got roastin ears or peas.

I go to the storekeeper. "Don't you work for Mr. Addison? Can't he let you have somethin?"

"He say he ain't got no more money."

I go on out of there and another store keeper say, "I'll let you have four or five dollars." I take that and make it go as far as I can.

I see the boss again and he say, "Do you know where we can

get you a job?"

"Maybe I can get one to the sawmill but I got the mules to take care of and that would mean I got to leave the crop." I have a late patch of corn or watermelon.

"Put the mules in the pasture. You can notice them and work at the sawmill and make your own way."

One year Mr. Addison got six of us hands a job to the stave mill. We was to go in the swamp and cut stave blocks to make barrels. It come a rain and the mosquitoes and the red bugs about eat us up. We work there two days. Then four or five of us ask Mr. Addison about lettin us have some money.

He went to raisin sand. "I got you all a job." We didn't say a word while he was talkin. He went to lookin from one to another.

I say, "Mr. Addison, you through?"

"Yeah, I'm through."

"Well, I'm goin to tell you the situation. We went to the swamp and the red bugs and the ticks and the mosquitoes are so bad down there we just can't stand it. Look like our blood sweet and they just eatin us up."

"Ah, well, if it's that a way you all can't work down there. I'll give you somethin to eat." He could have said, "Well, you go back or do without."

Pickin time. Maybe somebody brought a bale of cotton in from out my way. He seed it. He goin to hunt me then. "Ed, I come out the other day and seed you got a right smart of cotton."

"Yes, sir. It pretty thick."

"Don't you think you can scrape up a bale?"

"Yes, sir, if you want me to."

"I think you ought to get it and if you don't have a bale, well, you can put that up and if the weather come bad it won't get soiled."

Now he goes out to the crop. I had went fishin that day. "*My* crop is lookin pretty," Mr. Addison say to my wife.

"Yes, sir," she say and get mighty upsot by his sayin "my" crop.

I come home through town and he see me. "What you doing? Just setting around town?"

"No, sir, I done picked about three-quarters of a bale. It's pretty."

It come a storm and turn the cotton sort of gray. I pick some of that bad cotton. I put about three or four hundred pounds of that first pretty cotton I pick in the bottom of the wagon. Then I load the bad cotton on top. Now I'm ready to wind up my bale. I take about two or three hundred pounds of that good cotton and put it on top.

When I go to the gin I first gin the good cotton on top, then the bad cotton in the middle and then the pretty cotton on bottom. That slap the good cotton on both ends of the bale. When the man at the warehouse cuts a sample he'll give me a strict middlin grade and all the time I ain't got one in the center of the bale. I've done it many times.

By the latter part of September it's all picked. I gather my peanuts or whatever I've raised and take the rest of my cotton to the warehouse and get it ginned and baled. Now Mr. Addison can handle it and just as sure as you're livin he'll call it his'n. "*My* cotton, *my* corn, *my* crop." But he would do what he thought was right. Up to that time he was the best boss I had found.

After the crop was laid by, you couldn't hardly borrow a dime. I could usually get me a job workin for Mr. Burnett. There was just his thrasher to twenty-five or thirty farmers in the settlement.

Say you took up peanuts makin seventy-five or one hundred stacks in August and let them dry out about a month. You'd want them thrashed and you'd be runnin over there to his house beggin Mr. Burnett to come. All the rest would be doin the same.

Mr. Burnett would run the peanut picker hisself. To feed it he would hire me and Gene Daniels. He hardly ever lef a job less'n somethin got to pesticatin him, sickness or somethin bad. Thrashin peanuts is hard work. Me and Gene have done it many a time, from Monday mornin to Saturday night. If the wind was blowin, you'd have a nice time. You could set the picker where the wind blow the dirt to the side nobody workin on. But if it a still day the dust will settle so bad you'll have to stop.

Anyone subject with allergy or asthma couldn't take it. Some had goggles. And dusty. Ooh! You'll be so dusty you can't see nothin but your eyes when night comes.

I didn't have nothin but a tin tub. I'd have to heat up water, put it in the tub, and mix it with cool water, and try to get off that thick coat of dust stickin to my sweat.

It was hard to get a few peanuts thrashed because Mr. Burnett want at least half a day's work any place he took the machine.

Only about twelve or fifteen stacks of peanuts was what an old colored couple in our settlement had. One real hot September day we had already thrashed at one farm and nobody didn't want to stop by this old couple's place. But I tell Mr. Burnett, "There ain't no use passin them by." So he stop.

Me and Gene Daniels was the only colored workin that day. As soon as we stop, the old lady come out with a bucket of water. She pass the dipper around to all the white men. Then she pour what was left onto the ground. She didn't offer me or Gene or her husband nare drop.

She was a bright color and I knowed she attend services at the white folks' church. I reckon she thought she was better than the general run of the colored. Her husband was dark and he went to the colored church.

I don't remember what me and Gene Daniels said about her but it wasn't good.

Mr. Wesley Evans worked his daddy's one-horse farm and he was white but he was poor like me. I never knowed him to kill more than one hog a year. He'd make it go as far as he could.

"Ed," he say, "I got you all's baler. Mr. Huey Lindley" (he the overseer where I worked) "tell me you can turn out a bale of hay a minute with that."

"Well, I can put out a bale a minute if I can get people to throw it up to me fast enough."

"If you rush the job I'll pay you *good.*"

I didn't question about what he was goin to pay.

Next day we took the baler to the field where Mr. Evans had his pea vine hay. Crabgrass hay has sandspurs in it. That slow you down because the sandspurs stick you and get on your gloves. Velvet bean hay has a fur on it that get on your skin and stings you. That throw you back in workin some, 'cause you'll sure stop to scratch. But pea vine hay is soft to handle; it's near about like gatherin up clothes.

I felt good in them days. I had me a yellow, little old flop-up hat that I turnt wrong side out. I get up on this machine and went to cuttin the monkey and callin for hay. "Hay! More hay!" Fast as they could get it I'd yell, "Hay!"

The baler was the biggest ever I seed, "like the ones they use out west to bale alfalfa," Mr. Addison say. The biggest thing I had to do was to set the block. It went clean through the machine, cut the hay into a bale, and hit the ground with it.

I'll say they was about ten of us men, some white, some colored, workin that day. Them throwin hay from the stack up to the baler was the ones really workin and they got washed down in sweat quick. They sort of got mad with me 'cause I was workin them so hard. But the overseer was standin right there holdin his watch so they couldn't say much.

Two men was tyin out the bales, Mr. Evans and another white man was totin them off. The men was workin and the mules was trottin. How that hay went through the baler this day! It just kept a crawlin.

A man throwin hay to me say, "What you rushin for?"

We baled fifty-one bales of hay in one hour. I could have drug around there half a day and Mr. Evans would have had to pay us each fifty cents. The least I was expectin to get out of it was about two dollars. If there'd been a rain before we got it baled, this hay would have been more damaged than that.

Nobody knowed the secret 'cept me and Mr. Evans. He

didn't pay off Saturday night. Sunday mornin soon as I eat breakfast I walk by his house. It was about fifty yards off the road. He didn't come out so I walk on up the road over the hill, turnt around and come back by. I wanted the money but I didn't want to ask him for it. When I come back by, he come out.

He say, "Ed, I paid the rest of 'em ten cents and I'm gonna give you fifteen."

I couldn't hardly walk on off. I knowed Mr. Evans was a poor man just like me. But I was tryin to help him and make a little extra for myself at the same time.

The worstest thing about it was that some of my friends was sort of mad with me. Mr. Evans told the overseer so everybody knowed I didn't get nothin and then the crowd really laughed at me. I thought the joke was goin to be on all the rest of them but the joke fell back on me.

I sure knowed Mr. Evans was white. If I'd a said anythin, he would have said I was sassin him. If I had a been white like him, he'd a paid me more or whipped me one.

Every once in a while the white folks would come at you. Mr. Stanley—he was my closetest neighbor—tell Mr. Addison, "Ed is botherin me."

"What he doin to you?" Mr. Addison ask.

"Nothin."

"Well, then, how is he botherin you?"

"I'm afraid he's goin to."

Mr. Addison sent for me. "Mr. Stanley want me to get shut of you. He want you to move."

"I ain't botherin him no way."

"You ain't been goin in his yard gettin water? You ain't been foolin around his house?"

"No, sir."

Mr. Stanley was the white man told me he knowed my daddy. Every time I come down the hill from my house to the public road I had to go by his house. Settin on his porch, Mr. Stanley could see the back of the house of a colored family named Marsh. Beulah Marsh was about courtin size and some people thought Mr. Stanley was givin her money.

The Marshes bein the nearest colored family, I used to go there sometimes. I reckon Mr. Stanley thought I went there to court Beulah. But I didn't. Me and my wife was young and not too long married.

"Well, Ed," Mr. Addison say, "if I was livin out there where you is, I'd say stay. But I ain't out there. I don't want you to get hurt. You can go or you can stay."

"Mr. Addison, if you don't care, I'm goin to stay."

I goes to Mr. Stanley. He is about seventy years old but he could work good and plowed every day. I tell him, "I ain't goin to bother you and I don't want you to be afraid of me."

" 'Fraid of you? I'll take a pole and frail you!"

I had left Mr. Oakes because of Horace Martin, the white man that would lay down on my porch drunk. Now just when I had gotten in good with Mr. Addison, Mr. Stanley was wantin me to leave. Thinkin about movin on put me in mind of a rabbit. Zigzag, zigzag, dodgin one hunter then the next.

I goes back to Mr. Addison. "I wants to stay."

"Stay," Mr. Addison say. "I can't hire hands to please Stanley. I got to hire hands to please myself."

The next time I seen Mr. Stanley, he told me what I knowed all along was rufflin him. "I seen someone with Beulah on the back porch. Whosoever that was was puttin his hands between her legs."

"Well, it wasn't me."

Beulah moved and Mr. Stanley got to be a good friend. When my daughter Lottie started goin by his house to go to school his two old maid daughters would give her some biscuits or a baked sweet potato to carry in her lunch box.

7 My stepdaddy had a stroke and was paralyzed from the waist down. His stomach would blow out. So I took to helpin Ma by goin down there and drawin his water.

Mr. Brown's most regular visitor was Pastor Hill, our pastor at the Piney Grove Baptist Church for thirty years. He still visit the sick but he was old and sometimes he would forget where he was goin.

"How you like Dr. Grim, the root worker?" Mr. Brown ask Pastor Hill.

"That's a God-sent man," the preacher say. "He can cure anythin."

Dr. Grim was always talkin about what him and God would do, that the Lord had give him healin power. And that he could fix things between man and wife. He would tell a lady, "Clean your man off with a dishrag so he can't bother no other woman." A man he'd tell, "If a woman got you tricked so you can't go with another woman, throw a knife in the floor."

I try to get Mr. Brown to send for Dr. Durham, a real doctor. But Mr. Brown wouldn't have him. Him and Pastor Hill and Dr. Grim would set there talkin day after day.

White and colored around Rochelle would talk about the money old man Jackson Walker buried. Ma and Mr. Brown moved into a house behind where Mr. Walker had lived. They plowed deep and if they seed anythin that looked a little curious they'd dig. Once my stepdaddy plow up a stump with a cross on it. Him and Ma just knowed they had found the money. They never did, but my stepdaddy kept right on lookin for it until he move to Donald Clark's place and made two payments on a house there. Not long after that he had his stroke.

I would visit with him some and take him the news, such as what was going on at church.

Passin the time of day, I tell Dr. Grim about my trouble with Robert, my sister Rose's husband. Sober he was a pretty good fellow but anytime he got drunk he went to clownin and cuttin the crazy. He would wave his pistol around and want to walk over everybody else.

"If you bothers me again," I tell him, "I'm gonna shoot you." I borrow me a pistol from my brother Homer and had it a month before he took it back.

The fourth Sunday of the month I was standin pretty high up on the steps of the Piney Grove Baptist Church when Robert come and snatch me right off them. I reach for Homer's pistol. Then I member I had give it back. It was a good thing I didn't have one because I'd a sure popped it to him and I guess I'd a gone to the chain gang then.

"I come here to beg your pardon," Robert say.

"That ain't no way to beg my pardon."

After I tell Dr. Grim about this he say, "I can handle this. You got two pennies?" I give them to him. "Try to throw these pennies somewhere so they'll never get back together again. You'll have no further trouble with Robert as long as them pennies stay apart."

But he was wrong. My sister Rose was pregnant. One evenin her chillen come to my house and say Robert had kicked her in the stomach and knocked her down. We went to see at her and got Dr. Durham and he tell me it was most too late because her appendix busted but he'd do all he could.

Takin Rose to the hospital that Saturday mornin, I ask her did Robert kick her in the stomach.

"Don't you all bother him." She never did say he didn't do it.

That evenin they sent us word from the hospital that she had passed.

The doctor say, "If I'd a thought you had any money I'd a taken her to the hospital before."

"We don't have the money," I tell him. "But the hospital ain't as much as a funeral."

It was 1928. I didn't have one dollar. I had to go get my sister on a log truck. Comin back, I was ridin on the back of the truck with the casket. I didn't have no money to do no better for Rose but I could feel for her. When she was small it was pickin cotton just as fast as she could go. Pick, pick, pick. When she got up a little it was havin young ones and lookin after them and workin to feed them. Never one day in a flower bed of ease.

I said then if I ever got a chance without stealin from nobody I was goin to try to have somethin so if I want to put some of my folks in the hospital, or if somethin worse happened, I could put them away pretty decent.

Aaron married my wife's sister Bertha. He hadn't been in the family long when Robert come wavin a pistol at him. Aaron run in the house, got his shotgun, and rip the top off Robert's head.

I have heard Mr. Brown argue down a deacon who was swearin that before electricity was put over the country you could see hants. "There ain't nothin to that," my stepdaddy would say.

But in the fall of the year after he got sick he could see hants comin just at sundown. About three hundred yards from the house my stepdaddy was livin in was the colored cemetery. About the same distance the other way was an old white cemetery. "I don't think it the colored people botherin me. I believe it the white folks up there."

He got weaker and weaker. Ma had me to bring her some coins to put over his eyes when he died. He cry and say he don't want to go.

"You goin to be with us a while," Ma tell him. To me she say, "Death is the gateway to endless joy. But don't no one want to enter there."

He tell ma, "Go live with Ed."

That night he died.

In my heart I loved my stepdaddy some. Yet and still I don't think he treated me right. And when I was a boy I sure enough hated him. I used to say when I got grown I was going to kill him.

8 I was already poor in 1929 when I got my Model T—it was a 1926 model with no top. It near about got to where I couldn't buy groceries. Learnin myself to drive, I stayed in my car too much burnin gas and oil.

In Abbeville they knowed me at the courthouse and knowed I could drive. So I always had a driver's license. I couldn't read the signs but I didn't have to. Anyway, there wasn't many then. I knowed the roads for miles around because I had walked them and driv a wagon over them every which way.

When I got my car I had six bales of cotton seed, as good as cash, settin in my dinin room. Ten dollars a bale I sold them for and used it mostly for gas and oil for that car.

It had a short exhaust. Instead of the pipe bein bent like an elbow it hung straight down toward the ground from the manifold. It really stirred up the dust on dirt roads. I could drive up under the shelter and get out and look back and see the dust I'd raised way down the road.

Mr. Stanley would tell me, "Ed, you gonna kill yourself in that thing."

Lord knows my Model T was way too expensive for me to run. Durin the depression it was all you could do to eat. Only a few rich people in my section could buy a tag and gas to keep a car goin.

Mr. Stanley run out of gas one day. He park his Oldsmobile with practically new tires on the side of the road, get out, and say to his son, "Well, that did it!" The car set right there till it rotted.

One day me and Mr. "Red" Moore, a carpenter that had an old Model T, was walkin home from town. I ask him, "How come you walkin and you got a car?"

"I try to walk durin the week so Saturday and Sunday me and my wife can ride out to town and to church."

I was lucky. I swapped my Model T to Mr. Howard Bussell, the workinest man I ever knowed. He had four mules. What come up between them I don't know, but his son left him one year the first part of June, the busiest time. Mr. Bussell would take one mule to the field before sun and work that mule to nine or nine thirty. One of his daughters would bring him another and he'd hitch that one up and go till twelve. He'd take that one home hisself and stay just long enough to eat dinner. Then he'd take another mule to the field and stay till three or four o'clock. His daughter would bring him the fourth mule and he'd go as long as he could see.

His son was at his brother-in-law's. I talked with the son. He want to come back home just as bad as his daddy want him.

I ask, "Mr. Bussell, do you want your boy home?" You don't have nothin to do but go ask him."

He went and got his son. "I declare, Ed, you's a peacemaker." He brought a pretty mule to my house. "How 'bout tradin this mule for that car you got? I want to give it to my son."

I really didn't need a mule. "How about a cow? If I had me a cow and a churn and a dasher I'd swap you."

He trade his mule for two cows, one of them with a calf. He give me the one with the calf and brung me a churn and dasher. That's how I got rid of my Model T.

My struggle was on. Now that I didn't have any way to ride, I had to tote my baby whenever we went to church or off from home at night. Sometimes she'd be half sleepy and cryin. Later she used to ride on my back with her legs throwed about my waist. Walkin home one evenin, I looked down at her large thighs. I throwed her down. "I'm not totin you any more. You's about as big as I is." Lottie was five or six years old.

Wilcox County is dry but there are so many bootleggers they ought to wear badges to keep from sellin to each other.

Just like the milkman deliver milk in the daytime, a bootlegger will take whiskey around to his customers at night. The only bootlegger I ever knowed to deliver moonshine in the daytime was Police Chief Norton's son. He sold mineral water and he had five-gallon jugs of mineral water and of moonshine on his truck.

A heap of times the night policeman bought the moonshine from the still and delivered it. Either he would leave it at his customer's house or at another place, like a certain clump of bushes. Sometimes it would get stolen by someone who knew where it was delivered and was hidin nearby waitin for it.

The biggest bootleggers was almost always white. They got in with the police chief and paid him off. Most all of the colored who sold whiskey and had to go to jail would be particular the first night they got out but they'd go right back to sellin it. There's good money in it if you don't get caught.

Gordon Hope was a hustlin fellow and had a good hustlin wife. When they start sellin whiskey, Gordon made money and he spent it on nice furniture, a Rocket 88 Oldsmobile, and right smart of cows and hogs.

He was livin too good to suit his bossman, Mr. Peters. They was on shares and when Gordon had done finished layin by the crop, Mr. Peters driv up to Gordon's house with a revenue officer layin down on the floor of the back seat of the car. "Gordon," Mr. Peters say, "I want to buy some whiskey."

Gordon told him he didn't have none to the house, he'd have to go to the woods and get some.

Mr. Peters say, "Let's go."

They drove to the woods and Gordon got the whiskey. When he come back to the car the revenue officer sat up and arrest him. He went to the chain gang and Mr. Peters got both shares of the crop.

Once J. W. Cromer told me, "Ed, I'm goin to run off a charge tonight. You want to come over to my house?"

"I don't care if I do."

Two white fellows was at J. W.'s when I got there. I wouldn't have went if I'd knowed these fellows was in on it.

Time I got there one of them say, "Punch up the fire."

That's because moonshine is illegal. And if you do anythin to help, you're in on it and ain't likely to tell on nobody else.

My brother-in-law Vine had been tellin me that I didn't have sense enough to live, that I worked too hard. He made the bad mistake of tryin to sell moonshine without payin the police. They knowed he was sellin it and for about a year the police in Rochelle was tryin to catch him.

He would sell his booze and set around on the streets. But when the sheriff would come he'd run to me. One hundred dollars was what Vine was fined the second time he got caught. By mortgagin Bessie and her calf—the stock I swapped for my Model T—me and my wife paid the fine.

After that the law paid Vine's cousin eleven dollars to show them the hidin place. He took the law to the open well where Vine put the moonshine ready to sell after he stretch it with Clorox.

When Vine got caught he went to Uncle Tom, the root worker. He was a dirty little old man who kept his dogs right in the house with him. "Uncle Tom," Vine say, "I don't want to go to the chain gang."

"Take this and dress the courthouse steps with it and you won't go!" The stuff he give Vine looked like meal. When Vine couldn't get back to the courthouse, he want me to scatter it on the steps so he'd come clear. I was scared to do that.

The third time Vine got caught they wouldn't let us pay. I figured the judge just wasn't lettin us have him because he colored.

"Send a white person to get him," I told my wife.

Vine's wife was as ugly as you'll find them. She didn't want her husband goin to the chain gang so she went to a very rich lady at Sibbie who had a big farm and could use a hand.

"I'll get him if he can be got," the lady promise. She went to the judge and he say Vine had give a lot of trouble, he was hard to catch, and he was goin to have to serve some time to break him up from sellin.

Now that Vine was on the chain gang, he was doin farm work, plowin, choppin cotton, pickin cotton, pullin fodder, pullin corn, all the things he said I was so dumb for doin.

"How come I'm so dumb yet everybody comes runnin to me if they get in a tight?" I ask my wife. "I ain't never been locked up yet. I'm dumb in education. Some of the very people who keep runnin to me can read and write. Well, I can't. But still I wouldn't do some of the dumb things they do."

9 In 1929 Mr. Addison bought a tractor. He was the first man I ever knowed to have one. Right away he cut the fifteen men on his place down to four hands. It would be a favor to him, he say if I could get myself another job. That was the turrible year I worked on shares for Mr. Leslie Prince.

To buy food and to take care of the smokin and chewin me and my wife wanted to do while we was makin the crop, Mr. Prince said he'd loan me ten dollars a month. He would put it out, he say, but not all in cash, January through June, with interest at 15 per cent. He was aimin to make me take all the meat and syrup he could from his smokehouse.

Then, on shares, the boss furnish you with the land, mule, seeds, tools, and one-half of the fertilizer. I was to put out the other half of the fertilizer and all the labor.

Things went all right for a while. I was the best cotton picker there. Whenever Mr. Prince hire anyone to pick by the hundred-weight he said, "I want you to beat Ed pickin." The most I ever picked in an hour was one hundred and thirty-five pounds.

But hard work didn't get me nowhere. Mr. Prince wouldn't show me the papers the gin and the warehouse give him so I didn't know what the crop had brung and what my share should be. He took his share and all of mine and claim I owe him twenty-four dollars in addition.

In panic times ten dollars would buy a horse wagon full of groceries. You could buy a twenty-four pound sack of Twineida flour, a very good grade, for one dollar and fifteen cents, ten pounds of sugar for fifty cents, fifteen pounds of bacon for ten or fifteen cents a pound. A gallon of syrup would cost fifty cents and so would a peck sack of flour.

And usually I had a garden, either for myself or on halves with the boss, such as potatoes, squashes, onions, turnips, collards, cabbage, snap beans, butter beans, peas, Irish potatoes, tomatoes, and okra. Come summer my wife would put up seventy-five or eighty jars of blackberries, plums, watermelon rinds, apple preserves, and jelly. She raised chickens and I would have a sweet potato patch and a cane patch.

After the ten dollars a month furnish money was cut off in June it was best to be with a fellow that knowed you had to live through the winter too. A landlord would most likely want you and your family to have enough to eat if you was stayin on to make another crop. But if you wasn't he didn't care.

My wife want us to work for Mr. Prince because his tenant house had glass windows. When he come by our house he would smile and wave, wave and smile. She say, "I declare that is a nice man. I believe he would be a good man to work for."

I thought it would suit me because he said I could make a garden on halves. Before I had gathered much Mr. Prince acted friendly to some people, "Get anythin out of the garden you want." They cleaned it out. That made me a little dissatisfied. And my wife kicked because whenever I want to borrow Mr. Prince's mule to carry her to church on Sunday, he would say, "No, the mule should rest on Sunday."

Another reason I was dissatisfied was because I was a strong man behind a going mule. Mr. Prince figure my time worth the same as one of his boys. They was chillen at the time and quite natural they couldn't do a man's work.

Most white chillen went to school. But any landlord who was furnishin money to feed a colored tenant would expect him to take his chillen out of school to do what need doin on the farm.

By walkin over the farm all the time, Mr. Prince knowed if you was behind with anythin. After school and on Saturday he had his sons work for me. "Ed, what about takin the chillen over there to soda your cotton?"

The boys would walk over thirty acres of cotton carryin a

one-half gallon bucket of soda in one hand and droppin it with
the other. I'd follow along behind plowin the soda under. Whatever time the chillen spent helpin me I'd owe their daddy. I
didn't favor that.

After a year's hard work and makin a good crop I ask Mr.
Prince for a settlement. "I ain't got the books ready today," he
said. "I want to have a settlement when we get through gatherin
everythin." After I had even my late corn in the crib I went back
and he got out the book.

It didn't look to me like he could figure worth nothin—'bout
like me. I had made seven bales of cotton and two horse wagon
loads of corn, but Mr. Prince claim I hadn't made enough to pay
off my sixty dollars' furnish money and that I still owed him
twenty-four dollars.

He put the corn in the crib without weighin it. Velvet beans
was bringin a dollar a hundred pounds, and he took all of them.
And all the sweet potatoes.

"I tell you what I'm goin to do," he say. "I'll take your milk
cow for the twenty-four dollars."

Me and my wife had brung the cow and the calf I swapped
for my Model T Ford with us from the Addison place. We brung
two hogs and I had give Mr. Prince one to let me fatten the other
in the peanut field. He took both of them.

"No, I'm not givin the milk cow because it don't belong to
me, it belong to my wife."

"Well, you could just give me a mortgage on the cow and
carry her on with you."

I goes home and tell my wife, "Don't give no mortgage on
the cow. Don't give nothin on her."

My wife was more nervy about some things than I was. She
put a rope around the cow's neck and carry her to my brother's.
Then she make another trip there with the two little pigs she got
washin and ironin for her bosslady. Mr. Prince took my pig he
was lettin me fatten in his peanut field.

I goes back to him. He was settin on the steps to his porch.
"Mr. Prince, it don't look to me I owe you that much, not
twenty-four dollars."

He had give his boy a long knife. "David, bring me the knife," he say.

I walk on off. After that he just kept a comin to my house late at night, way in the night, and wantin me to go out in the field with him "to talk it over."

"How come you can't talk it over here to the house? We ain't got to go in the field to talk over no settlement. I didn't come to your house late in the night to get this place."

"We'll go out where it cool."

"It cool enough for me in here."

I seed there wasn't no use talkin. If it had been fair as a lily and he'd said it was rainin and I'd said no, he'd said I was disputin his word. And if you had met him you'd a thought he was the best man in the world. He wouldn't pass colored or white except he'd speak and smile, speak and smile.

He'd go to the table every mornin and say a long prayer over it and then he'd come right out of that house and take every bit of bread out of your mouth. And he'd raise more sand than forty lawyers. "Now I'm goin to the field, boys, and it'll pay you all to come on." He'd plow until about eleven and then quit. "You colored can stand the sun."

When it come a big rain he'd say, "Boys, let's get the cross saw and cut stove wood." I had a pile of stove wood I don't know how high in the yard. So did the other tenants and Mr. Prince. He'd get his wood cut that a way without payin for it.

One mornin come a rain. "Let's cut some stove wood."

I say, "I ain't cuttin nare nother stick of stove wood for nobody. I've got enough stove wood to last me. What I'm worried about is gettin something to cook with this I got."

After that I'd walk about when it was rainin. He talked around. "Well, Ed's a good hand but he sure is mean." I wasn't mean. I just wasn't goin to cut no more stove wood. When you got enough of anythin you don't need no more.

When I was fixin to leave, Mr. Prince ask me, "Ed, have you found a place to live?"

"Yes, sir, up there with Mr. Motley."

"Motley at Rochelle?"

"Yes, sir."

I went to Mr. Motley to get his wagon to move. "I think our deal is off, Ed. Mr. Leslie Prince just been here and he say you're a good hand but you're mean and your wife is sick and your little girl is too small to do anythin."

I didn't know what to do. I had stayed in my place and lived in my bounds. You had to be mighty sharp then to make it for your folks. Mighty sharp and straight humble. If you wasn't, it'd make you have ulcers. You could get 'em from bein humble and from not bein humble enough.

One thing you was workin for was so the white man would say, "He's a good nigger." Then the others would let you alone. If one say you steal, whether you steal or not, if somethin is missin you took it.

Things was burdenin me. I walked back from Mr. Motley's towards Mr. Prince's. When I come to the black gum tree which was still scarred up from a lynchin that took place when I was a boy, I set down to study this thing out. The trouble was I hadn't left Mr. Prince when his other two tenants left. They was smarter than me.

When one of them seen what our boss was like, him and his wife and two chillen cleared out just before layin by time, about July fourth. Me and Emmett, the other tenant, was in the barn. Mr. Prince come by and say, "That lazy nigger is leavin. If anybody else want to go they're at liberty." The tenant leavin told us he suspicion the boss's bookkeepin. He went to pickin cotton by the hundredweight and made money.

Emmett stay till the cotton all picked and the corn gathered and we was balin hay. It was the last of October when him and Mr. Prince fell out. We had finished everythin but strippin cane. "Ed, if you'll stay," Mr. Prince say, "I'll give you what I been aimin to give you and both the others."

He didn't give me nothin but plenty of trouble. I reckon that's what he was goin to give them and he decide he'd give it all to me.

It took me two days to strip the cane and take it to the mill.

All one day I chop the wood for cookin it. So that was three days' work. Mr. Prince wasn't promisin me money for helpin with the cane but I was supposed to get half the syrup.

I just beginnin the fourth day's work when a colored gentleman, a butcher, come out from Rochelle and bought a cow. He had got old. If I help him butcher this cow he'll give me the tripe, the head, the tail, and the feets. So I goes to Mr. Prince. It was early in the mornin and he was at the table prayin. I had to wait the longest for him to get through, then I ask him could I help butcher the cow. "Go, if you want to."

After we butcher the cow I jump over the fence and taken what meat the butcher give me to my wife. We was glad to get it. Then I goes right back to the sugar mill and ask Mr. Prince what do he want me to do. "Nothin, you quit and went to helpin somebody else."

He had promised to pay me in syrup. Now he didn't want me to have any. So I ask him to pay me in money. He turnt me off. I ask him to let me cut him a cord of wood for an overall jacket to wear the comin winter. "No. I don't need no wood cut. I can tie a string around my plantation and me and my boys can live in it for twelve months."

The way I look at it, all our work—mine and the other tenants'—was piled up around him.

Soon after that we left there. My wife was singin and bouncin Lottie on her knees.

> *"Ought's a ought,*
> *All for the white man*
> *None for the nigger."*

10 "Where is the game tonight?" many men that went to town Saturday evenin would ask at the café. Sometimes we'd play in the back end of the café, or in a home out from town or in the woods. Before bolita come in so strong, all of us, the hands from our settlement, the colored that come to Rochelle from the little towns around, and the trustees from the county chain gang farm would be lookin for a skin game. It's called skin because it can skin you and it really will.

In my young days the white folks call our frolics "mullet suppers." "Ed, don't go to the mullet supper 'cause you'll get killed."

These frolics would begin around eight o'clock Saturday night, just as quick as you could get from town with all the fixins. You'd double the money you had in them and most all the time you'd sell clean out. There would be fried mullet sandwiches, all various soft drinks, fried potatoes, homemade ice cream, cigarettes, and cigars. A bootlegger would come and sell stump liquor.

Many mullet suppers was give for the church. The pastor would ask the members to raise money to buy benches or to do anythin wantin to be done. If you made as high as ten or fifteen dollars you could put about seven or eight in your envelope and keep the rest for yourself.

When I worked on shares on Mr. Leslie Prince's place me and the other tenants would invite the hands from other farms in the settlement and we'd have a big time. Out of that crowd some of them could pick a guitar. For a while we had one man could blow a harp good. You could dance to pattin hands. Or shimmy or do the Monkey or the Charleston.

Even the big church folks—deacons, too—would jump with

the music: "It ain't really dancin if you don't cross your feet."

Sometimes we'd have gamblin inside the house around a table with a flambeau for light. That's a Coca-Cola bottle filled with kerosene with a rag twisted down in it. Light the rag and it will burn just like a lamp without a chimney. It will smoke but you can see by it.

If the women folk wanted to go to bed, or if the house where the mullet supper was at was too small, the men would go outside and build a fire of lighterwood roots and play by it. Mostly money was so scarce that a fellow would get in the game with a few pennies or a big box of matches. If there was enough money in the skin game, we'd play till about three o'clock Sunday afternoon. Some would play awhile and sleep awhile.

Sometimes the law would catch us, lock us up, and charge us ten dollars apiece. A lot of people prowl the roads Saturday night. After cars come in, a fellow that went broke in Rochelle would leave there and run up on a game in the country or try it in another town.

On Saturday night in these little towns the day policeman and the night policeman would stay together. The night policeman in Abbeville was a bootlegger. When the policemen found us, if it was they moonshine we had, they'd take a drink. If they hadn't sold it to us and we heard them comin, we'd get shut of it. Then maybe one of them would walk up to the game and say, "Give me two of them." We'd hand him two dollars. "Play all you want to, but don't you all make too much noise." They'd go back to town.

My wife didn't much like me to play, especially when the skin game was at our house, because it's a violation of the law. But some of us played right regular.

There never was a party without Curtis Rogers. He was a young fellow that plowed every day and had a nice-lookin wife and a houseful of chillen but one of his knees was bent in like it was knock-kneed. His wife was the only lady I ever knowed to have two babies that wasn't twins in the same year. The rest of the men had been noticin that Curtis would lock his wife up in his house and then he'd come on and want to dance with everybody else's wife.

We had talked about this out in the field. More than me felt the same way, but it fell my lot to do somethin about it.

Curtis come and commence dancin with my wife. "Curtis, you won't bring your wife where no other man can dance with her. I don't want you dancin with my wife."

He got mad. "It look like you tryin to get hard."

"No, I stays hard."

He run out the door. A friend come and tell me, "Curtis gone home to ring a shell." That way in place of the shot scatterin they all stay together and bore a hole like a bullet.

When he come back I was standin just outside the kitchen door behind the chinaberry tree. It was dark but not too dark to see he had a gun in his right hand. When he start by me I grab his gun with my left hand and hit him across his head with my gun. I got down on him. He did get his hawk bill knife out his pocket, but he couldn't get it open.

Someone look out the window and seen us and holler, "They fightin out there." That drawed out the crowd. Mr. Addison had sent his overseer because too many of his hands had been gettin hurt at our frolics here lately. He come runnin with a flashlight. "Give me that gun."

I give him Curtis's shotgun. He broke it down and we seen Curtis had rung a shell. "Give me yourn." I didn't want to. I try to walk on off. Mine was a 32 Smith and Wesson, a real troublemaker. "Give it to me."

"You going to give it back to me?"

"Yeah."

I give it to him.

Curtis didn't try dancin no more that evenin.

Mr. Leslie Prince's stepson, Stuart—he was totin a stone jug of whiskey—and his two brothers come wantin to get in the game. These young white fellows had just turned courtin age, anywhere from sixteen to twenty. By the game bein on their daddy's place, I reckon they thought they could just take it over.

When they first come to our games we figured we'd win some money out of them. But they had took up a bad habit. When one of them lose all his change he'd take a twenty dollar bill out of his pocket, lay that down, and say, "Play in that."

I'm bettin a quarter. The whole story is I will go broke before I can win his twenty dollars. He will take our money and leave.

And if he ain't winnin, this is how he'll do. Say he owes me twenty-five cents, and that one twenty-five cents, and the next one, and on like that. He'll owe us about four or five dollars and he'll say he ain't at liberty to cash his bill. He'll walk right on out without payin nobody. Gamblin is a violation to the law. You can't collect a gamblin debt.

The last time the Prince boys flash a twenty dollar bill we had made up amongst ourselves we wasn't goin to play with them no further than their change went. If they want to be a bunch of crooks we wanted to get shut of them.

Stuart Prince come playin drunk with plenty of scratch in him. Long Boy was settin in his car. "What ya doin?" Stuart ask Long Boy and haul off and slap him. Two hundred pounds was what Long Boy weigh, most of it muscle, and he was nervy with it. But he didn't do nothin. He knowed better than to hit a white man.

Long Boy had had many fights with the colored in our settlement. "I don't mind fightin," he would say, "and I don't mind dyin." Everybody who come up against him knowed it was either kill or get killed.

"That's my nigger," the doctor's widow Long Boy rent land from would tell the police chief. "Let him alone. If he done anythin, I'll pay for it." In them days if you was a good worker, your boss folks would get you out of many things unless you got in it with the white people.

The big folks in town was payin the chief's salary. What they said went. So Long Boy was as free as a white man to knock and slash amongst the colored. Mighty few of the colored would carry him to jail unless the fight come up in town. Then the police would sometimes take him to court. But if the fight was in the country, it never was said nothin about.

Long Boy'd knock a small man away from his money and take it. Three times he hop on a little biddy colored guy named Hot Papa. The police didn't do nothin about it because the chief wasn't aimin to tangle with Long Boy's bosslady.

But it wasn't just her. It was Long Boy, too. I reckon that from slavery on up there have been some people that would stand up for theyselves. The white people didn't run over him as bad as they did the other colored.

Say Long Boy would go to town Saturday and do his devilment and get away from there and go home before the chief could arrest him. The chief would talk like this, "I ain't goin out there tonight and mess with old Long Boy. I'll be out there the first of the week." Monday he'd go, "Long Boy, I'm here to arrest you for cuttin up Saturday."

"Go on back to town," Long Boy'd tell him. "After I finish workin this evenin I'm comin down there and we'll straighten it out. I ain't goin to jail."

He had a big red horse and a good buggy and after he finish workin he'd go see the chief. Now you may think I'm tellin a story but that's the truth.

It had got so wouldn't nobody invite Long Boy to a skin game. But if he knowed where it was, there was no way to keep him out. Everythin was lovely as long as he was winnin. Whenever that change he'd go to fightin and tear up the game.

So didn't nobody cry when Stuart slap Long Boy.

Soon as Stuart set down he come right out with his twenty dollar bill. Time Curtis Rogers seed it, he say, "I ain't gonna play with you in that kind of money cause you ain't gonna play fair."

Stuart figure he had got holt of the weakest somebody there. Nobody, colored or white, thought Curtis would fight. But you can't depend on somebody being scared by him bein crippled. Long Boy was scared to hit Stuart. Me, too, but not Curtis. He grab the whiskey jug and hit Stuart Prince acrost the head with it and knocked him out.

We stood there. You could have heard a rat pissin in high corn. After a while the other Prince boys stand their brother up between them and carry him out the door. Curtis left from there that night. In them days if you hit a white man you had to take to "Mr. Bush" to stand your bond. I mean you had to move on.

"Carry the game to the woods," my wife beg me. She was bad worried would them white boys come back. "Go on way from here. I ain't aimin to be no widow."

I sure thought it would be best for everyone to go home but Long Boy say, "Shoot! Let's play."

We was not as worried as my wife because we had been drinkin Block and Tackle. That's stump—the white folks mostly call it Moonshine or White Lightnin—that a bootlegger like Mr. Ted Cross, the police chief in Abbeville, would try to stretch with cigar ashes, or Clorox, or red pepper. That would mess it up. You could drink it on this block and walk to the next and tackle anybody you met. We drunk a lot of it at our frolics.

"Let them Prince boys come," Long Boy told my wife. "If they come back, tell them we waitin for them down to the large oak by the branch."

I figured they a little too drunk to come back.

Long Boy was just talkin big. It wasn't whiskey that made him act up. It was money.

It had got so he didn't even bother to carry a gun. If he went broke in the skin game and wouldn't nobody lend him money, he'd just get him a chair or a piece of wood and bust it over someone. Leastways anyone colored. Then the man he took money from would most likely set there and beg him for some of it back.

His bosslady was able to keep him out of trouble till him and Hot Papa tangled. Just before we left my house Hot Papa had showed up lookin for a game.

We went down by the branch. The water was clear and cool and the honeysuckle smelled just as sweet.

"I ain't lookin for the law here tonight," Long Boy say.

Hot Papa tell me by him workin for the city he had come

to stand in good with the law. How come this and how come
that going on amongst the colored, his bossman would ask him.
While he talkin we clear us off a place and build us a lighterwood
fire, "not too high," Daimon Lee say. "We got to see the cards
but we don't want to be seed from the road." We call ourselves
keepin clear of the law.

Daimon was a trustee so he had a range and didn't have to
be under a gun all the time. The cap'n of the county farm would
turn the convicts he liked loose Saturday evenin to gamble and
shoot dice and have fun just like any free person.

Fun is good for everybody. It rest your mind from your daily
tasks. When Daimon first come didn't nobody know him. He
got up somethin funny to tell us—stories about what happen on
the chain gang—so he could join in. In two or three weeks we
had got use to him and we was lookin for him to come.

It was easy for him to have a girl friend because he could
steal things from the camp to give her. Or, he'd bring a bar of
soap or a piece of meat from camp to trade for money to gamble
with. If he'd win he'd have somethin to carry back to the camp
to play skin with there.

All of us raised up in Wilcox County knowed the story of
Hot Papa's daddy. But Daimon didn't. Hot Papa say, "My
daddy never play hisself but he always around the skin game
with money. If you went broke he would take what you had in
pawn, your pants or ring, hat, your watch, anythin you had
worth money.

"One night—I was ten years old—this fellow come to the
game wearin a pair of Sunday pants give him by his bossman.
The fellow went broke and pawned his pants. Daddy give him
a pair of raggedty pants to wear home. His bossman ask, 'Why
you wearin them raggedty old overalls Saturday evenin? What
happen to that blue serge suit I give you?'

"The fellow told him, 'I lost my pants in the skin game and
I want you to go get them for me.'

"His bossman come to our house and say to my daddy, 'Give
me my nigger's pants.'

" 'I have three dollars in them pants. Give me three dollars and I'll give you the pants.' The bossman slam out of the house with no further words.

"Saturday evenin when Daddy and Ma go to town, Ma notice this same bossman in the company of Mr. Cross. He is a man known to have killed several men, some white, some colored, for pay. He shoot my daddy down. About three years from that day Mr. Cross come to be the chief of police of Abbeville, Georgia, and his brother a policeman."

While Hot Papa talkin to Daimon, Daimon seein do he fancy Long Annie. She was Long Boy's sister and not as bad about fightin as Long Boy but she could sure drink liquor. Not ugly but I wouldn't say she was pretty. She weigh about one hundred and sixty pounds and she tall and dark-skinned and have pretty good hair and two gold teeth.

Her clothes wouldn't be right. And if a man want to be with her, well, he'd be with her. Everybody claim Long Annie would win more money than a man could because men wouldn't watch her hands as close. She had limber fingers and could really handle cards in a slick way.

"You got dishpan hands," Long Boy tell her. "Shoot! You grab a plow all day or hoe cotton all day and Saturday night your hands be stiff."

That night Long Annie was the dealer. The top card belong to her. Every other one playin scoop him a card out of the deck. The first card she turn was a queen. That what Long Boy helt. It's called head peckin when a player fall the first time the dealer turn a card.

"Hot dam!" Long Boy say. "That dam queen ain't no good. It no good. I'll never play another." Long Boy lose his money to everyone he had bet his queen was deeper in the deck than the card they holdin. "I'm gonna stop you, you won't never take nothin from nobody else."

You can't hardly win at skin if you don't know how to carry the cub. Not unless you're overlucky. Carryin the cub is stealin the cards that match the one you're holdin. That way when the dealer turn the cards there won't be any in the deck to make you fall.

The best way to do is to get two alike cards while you're shufflin. A really smart player will sometimes get three cards. Some people got hands like a piano player. They can fool your eyes out. You can look right at they hands and can't see them do nothin. A smart man with smart hands will put those cards he got when he was shufflin at the very bottom of the deck.

That's the best way. Not many can do it. Most will hide it up they sleeve or wherever they can. Then somehow they got to get it back to the pile turned over by the dealer.

Sometimes before the game you can make agreements to help a buddy. You can take your bare foot and touch your buddy with a card in your toes. He'll reach under the table with his hand and get it. He'll try to put it back or hold it to use in the next game. Mostly at the beginnin of a game "All cubs barred" was announced. It sure gonna bring about a fight if somebody notice a player has got a cub out.

If Long Boy steal a card from the deck and he knowed I saw him sneak it back in there he'd wink. That mean don't say nothin now but when the game is over I'll give you back the money you bet on my card. Keep bettin. If I keep right on bettin even though I knowed some of the cards of a suit was out, I'd be called a booster. I'm makin like everything is O.K. to keep the others bettin.

After the game I could ask Long Boy for the money I spent boostin. And he was due to give me a little extra. Most anybody else would hand that money right over. But Long Boy might not. He was nervy and knowed I didn't want to tangle with him. "I didn't carry no cub," he'd say.

So we had all got tired of Long Boy's doins.

Long Annie dealt again and Long Boy bet more than before.

Daimon was broke. "Lemme borrow some," he ask Hot Papa.

"I wouldn't give a bitch a bone if she was comin down the street with seven puppies." But just then Hot Papa rake in three

dollars. He threw a quarter to Daimon and he paid me for the
light I had put out to play by at home before the Prince boys
come. "Thank you," I told Hot Papa because he didn't have to
do that.

Daimon pick up the quarter and kiss it. "Stick with me,
Martha." He call the name of his girl friend. When his card fall
and he lose the quarter, he call out, "Martha is mad! I can't win
nothin."

Now Long Boy went broke. "Lemme have some of that
change," Long Boy say to Hot Papa.

"No. I been drinkin on credit. The man want money."

Long Boy grab this long, burnin pine root out of the fire and
circle it above his head. Then he tried to hit Hot Papa with it.
I tell him, "Friend, don't do that. Don't do that." He put it
down.

Long Annie shuffled the deck, hand the cards to Daimon to
cut, and turn over the first card. Long Boy was still tryin to get
in the game, "Lemme have some,"

"Go way," she say. "You's hard luck to the world."

There was about twelve dollars in the game. There wasn't
nobody sayin a word. You could hear every quiet sound in the
woods. A game like that is nervous anyhow. That's why a heap
of players will put they gun right by they money. The one settin
side you will steal your money out from under you if he can.

Hot Papa didn't have no pistol that nobody knows about.
But he had a long card—one that stay in the deck a long time
—and everybody was bettin on him. They really quiet, hearts
a thumpin.

Hot Papa had toted a bottle of Heart Cologne to the game.
He stand up, pull it out his pocket, and rub some on his hands
and on his money.

"That ain't good for nothin but pourin it on your sweet-
heart," Long Boy say.

"Yeah? It bring me luck in the game every time I use it."

One after the other fall. There was plenty of cussin. Hot
Papa had the best card, so he got the money.

"Give me some," Long Boy tell him.

"I wouldn't give a crab a crutch to walk across a wet pussy," Hot Papa say. He draw his money up close to him.

That did it. Long Boy grab a piece of wood and bring it down on Hot Papa. The blood run down Hot Papa's face and into his eyes. He was tryin to balance hisself. "Long Boy, I'm goin to get you."

Hot Papa leave his money and goes off. Long Boy pick it up and say he tired and got to go to bed.

Sometimes the man winnin would go to the café. Then he'd have to set the whole crowd up to a drink because they'd figure he had all they money. But this night it didn't work that way. Didn't nobody follow Long Boy.

About three o'clock Sunday afternoon Long Boy was all dressed up, bull skatin around with the ladies at the café. It didn't have but one way out and that was the front door. Hot Papa walk up to it and call, "Long Boy!"

Long Boy look around and Hot Papa told him, "Here it is." The pistol done the rest of the talkin. Three shots was the end of Long Boy.

Soon as Long Boy fell to the floor Hot Papa walk up to him and taken the money out of his pocket. He count out what Long Boy owe him.

"Here your change." Hot Papa rain nickels and dimes down on Long Boy.

Many people say Long Boy was killed with the chief's gun. There were people that claim when Hot Papa leave the skin game he went to the police chief and told how Long Boy jumped on him for the fourth time. The chief could have said, "Well, why don't you kill him?"

"I ain't got no pistol."

"Suppose you was to borrow one?"

Hot Papa left there and never was heard tell of again.

About a week later me and my brother Homer was in town. He ask the chief, "Did you all ever catch the fellow that killed Long Boy?"

"No," he say. "Who in the hell want to catch him?"

The evening Long Boy died the overseer come to my house, I reckon to talk about the killin. He give me the gun he taken from me and offer me Curtis's. I knowed Curtis hunted for food. "Give Curtis his'n. All I wants is mine."

The overseer say, "Ed, you missed killin you a nigger and for free. I don't hardly think you'd have even got jail with him carryin on with your wife."

I tell him, "No. I don't never want to kill a man unless'n I just have it to do to keep him from killin me."

After that I didn't have no better friend than Curtis. I often thought if I'd a killed him I'd a lost a good friend. Mr. Stuart Prince didn't come back the night Curtis hit him. But Curtis was scared. He lit out for Cordele, Georgia, where he live today.

When the welfare come they open his leg up at the clinic and straighten him. Now he can walk down the street just as nice as anybody. He's as old as I is but he still calls hisself a hard sport with the ladies.

11 Durin the worst of the panic people was walkin to and fro, up and down the highway. Men would come into the settlement and go from house to house beggin for somethin, anythin to do. The white people could get a yard cut for thirty cents and hedges clipped for twenty-five cents.

In 1930, I sold my cotton for five cents a pound. My share of that was two and one-half cents. A man who didn't have no regular way of gettin food had to steal or starve.

Bob Abbott couldn't get a farm. Him and his wife and chillen—five or six—didn't have enough to eat. I come acrost him one day setting on the railroad.

"How is your people?"

"Down with the measles."

"What you settin here for?"

"I'm scared of the measles."

But he caught them and died. While he was livin him and his people went hungry. But the day he died I went by the leakin, broken-down house he was livin in and you couldn't hardly get in his yard for the people bringin ham, shoulders, flour, meal. It was all stacked up.

Just about the time of the panic the tractor come in strong. At first it didn't have rubber tires, just cleats that would catch in the ground. The driver would only work in the middle of the field and men with mules went in the corners and along the fences, where you couldn't turn a tractor around.

In just a few years the tractor improved so much it put the mule out of business. The landowner was quick to take a likin to the tractor. With it he would have no people to feed, no doctor's bills or houses to repair, and no mules to feed. He could buy fertilizer with the money he used to pay hands.

Men started walkin the roads looking for a farm, for a dry place to sleep, and a place to raise somethin to eat. Mr. So and So, they'd tell me, has got a tractor and I got to move. Some would walk weeks lookin for a farm.

With people travelin you didn't know what they did. They could be robbers or murderers. From the highway you could see my house settin back about two hundred yards. White or colored, anybody who ask, my wife would feed.

A rough-lookin, short-built fellow come while me and my brother-in-law was cuttin cord wood for the gin. "Do you have any food done cooked you could give me?"

By him seemin in a hurry I wonder could he have been into somethin and runnin away. We give him some biscuits and syrup. He talk big. "This all you got to eat?"

"If you'll stay and help us cut some cord wood this evenin, we'll pay you and give you some supper too."

"No. I don't work for nobody."

"Well, get the hell on down the railroad," I say.

He stop and set down like he wasn't goin. I say to my brother-in-law, "Vine, go get the shotgun." Finally, when Vine come with the gun the man walk on down to the railroad, but he didn't hurry.

One day my granddaughter answer a knock at the back door. "It's a white man out there!" She run to me when she seed him.

I goes to find what do he want. Together with him bein white, what scared my granddaughter, I think, is that he was bearded and had a long, poor face. Do we have any food to give him? "How many eggs can he eat?" my wife ask.

"About seven."

She cook them and fry him some bacon and make him some hot biscuits and a pot of coffee. I put a quart of buttermilk in front of him. There was syrup and butter on the table. He finished every bit of it. Then he come and set down in the front room. "If I had a place to lay down now and go to sleep, I'd be all right."

I was afraid to keep him.

We was havin a dry spell and I had been haulin water from Abbeville, where he come from. I decided to haul water from Rochelle because if I carry him there he wouldn't be passin by my house again.

An old, old gentleman come one cold winter night. He was raggedty and patched every which a way. After he got thawed out by the fire we was settin there talkin. I ask him where was he travelin to.

"Florida."

"Why you walkin way to Florida?"

"The one I love is down there and I'm goin to get married."

"Married?"

"Yeah."

"Well, I believe if I had got as old as you is I wouldn't take a wife."

"Yeah, all of them tell me that. But they just like you."

"How's that?"

"They're settin up side of theirs."

One day in Hoover times comin home from Kramer along the railway track, I walk up on a fellow sitting in a dugout.

He was travelin to Savannah, and I say, "I'm goin on down about a mile. We can walk along together." He was carryin a bundle of clothes tied up in a bed sheet. When we got nearly to the turnoff for my place we come on a dead rabbit the train had run over. The man grabbed this rabbit just like it had been alive and was goin to run.

I tell him to my knowin the dead rabbit had been there for three days, if not longer.

He helt it up and smelt it. "That ain't nothin," he say. "It ain't ruint. It will help me travel."

When he got to the railway trestle he stop and wash the rabbit and I reckon he eat it because when I left he was buildin a fire.

One Saturday about ten or twelve men, white and colored, was workin on my place with the peanut picker. We didn't get through until near sundown. I had about four tons of hay to haul in before the rain come. "Who will help me haul in my hay?"

All of them holler, "Not me, not me."

A white man named George spoke. "I will," he say. The next mornin before day he come back with a truck and woke me up. "I'm ready to help you." By eight o'clock that mornin we had it all in. I paid him five dollars.

Him and his wife busted up and he leave and stay off one or two years. Then one night about twelve o'clock someone knock and call my name.

"Who is it?" I ask.

"George. Don't you know I help you haul in your hay that Sunday mornin?"

I open the door.

He told me to get up and make a fire. Me and him set and talk. He told about drivin a big transfer truck haulin produce from Florida to Atlanta and how he was goin to bring me some beans. I was settin up there believin him. Once I ask did he want to take off the overcoat he was wearin and he say no.

"Ed, would you give me a quilt and let me stretch out here in front of the fire?" I didn't hurry about answerin and he brung up the hay again. "You know I did you a favor."

The colored didn't go to the white and the white didn't go to the colored to spend the night. I ask myself why he doin it? I give him the quilt.

My wife say, "If you go to sleep, I'll stay woke."

We both go to sleep. When we knowed anythin it was day. I built another fire. Soon as he woke, George say, "Let's go down to the barn." We walk out there. "Ed, I been tellin you a bunch of stories. The reason I had to tell you that, I didn't want your family to be scared. I want you to do me a favor."

"What is it?" I ask.

"I want you to pull off your clothes and give them to me. This is a right new suit I got on. If you can get the letters out of it, you can wear it; if you can't, burn it up and get shut of it."

He pull off his coat. He was wearin a gray khaki chain gang suit.

"I'll try to find you some." So I goes to the house and get my one white shirt and my one pair of Sunday pants. I tell him, "Put this on." He change into my clothes and come back to the house to wash his face and comb his hair. He look nice.

"In two weeks time you'll hear from me." I never did.

I never turnt nobody down, white or colored. One mornin we had eat but my wife hadn't taken the dishes off the table. I was down at the barn when I seed this young colored gentleman go in my house. I walk up there. My wife had set him down at the table.

"Get up," I tell him.

"What's the matter?" my wife ask.

"I'm tired of feedin these loafers. Everybody come by want me to feed them."

My wife had filled the young man's plate. He stood up. "Please, mister, let me eat. Anythin that you see on me you can have for this breakfast. I got a good belt."

"Take it off then." He give me the belt and set down. I could see he was hungry. I commenced to feelin sorry for what I had did and I couldn't get that out of my conscience no way.

Helpin your neighbors was different. One lady thank me still. Her husband runned away and lef her with three chillen. Out in the country sometimes it was hard for a lady to get a job. A lot of the white people cook for theyselves.

The last time I seed this lady she grab me and hug me and told some of 'em at the Piney Grove Church Homecoming, "This man helped me when I couldn't help myself. He let me have food out of his garden and out of his kitchen to feed my chillen and I love him for it."

In panic times if you couldn't get a job and make enough to feed yourself and them in your family not able to work, you'd have to figure another way to live.

McLeod was a born burglar. He would steal the sweetnin out of a ginger cake or a thing so minor you wouldn't miss it but he'd always take somethin. It could be a spool of thread. Soon as he got it he'd carry it across the road and give it to someone there.

If there was somethin particular you didn't want him to take, it was best to say so.

We had about seventy-five chickens my wife had raised that bunched theyselves up on the east side of the house in the shade. One time me and my wife come back from town and driv up in our yard and there was McLeod settin on the porch lookin at the chickens.

Since Mac was a known chicken thief I walk right straight to him, "Don't bother my wife's chickens."

"Well, I'm glad you told me not to get them 'cause I was just thinkin about sackin them up."

"I'll help you out any way I can if you don't bother them."

That night he went to his mother-in-law's chicken house and help hisself to as many as he could get in two big sacks without smotherin them. Some of them was stickin they heads out of the holes he had cut in the sacks.

The next mornin he come to my house and 'minded me I say I'd help him. I took him in my wagon to Rochelle, where he try to sell them chickens on the street. Some he took ten, fifteen, or twenty cents apiece for.

How come he to sell them so cheap was because they was frizzly chickens—with feathers curly like a curly-headed man. When they young they look very pretty with curly feathers all over, but they molt and get to look near about half naked.

They scratch a lot. I always said they was scratchin for a livin. But many folks claim they was very good for scratchin up a conjuration somebody had put down in your yard.

Frizzly chickens is no different from any other chickens once you get the feathers off. But people don't like to eat them. Even at such a cheap price Mac was told, "I don't want them buzzards."

Mac come to spend two or three days with his sister so he could see what his brother-in-law, Rogers Hollis, had. The main thing was one milk cow. Mac got some men's shoes and ties them on the cow's feet so Rogers won't be able to follow her tracks. After Mac lead the cow to the railway tracks he take off the shoes and walk her from Burnham's Bay to Vienna, Georgia, about twenty miles.

He goes to the hands on a big farm. They was goin to buy the cow for seven dollars and butcher it and divide the beef amongst them. But before they could make up the money the law come and arrest McLeod. The judge sentence him to twelve months. If he didn't steal somethin from the jail, I would be surprised.

After Mac was in jail awhile Mr. Hyatt Wilcox paid his fine and got him out. Mr. Wilcox would not pay him in cash but let him take up his wages in groceries at the store.

Saturday night Mac was in the habit of takin up enough groceries for two or three people. Then he'd go right out behind the store and sell what he'd got for cash. If he had took up one dollar's worth of groceries, he'd sell them for fifty cents or even twenty-five. After pilin up a big debt at the store he runned away.

The first I knowed McLeod was back my brother driv up to my house and call, "Hey, Ed, here Mac! He want me to carry him over to Miss Estelle's." That was his mother-in-law. "You want to go with us?" I was settin in the bathtub and told them no. It was Saturday evenin and he had slipped back on the Seaboard train that run through there then to see his wife.

Somehow the white folks got in the winds of McLeod bein back. I was livin on Mr. Addison's place in Kramer in a house that white people had once lived in. It had glass windows and a narrow porch with a rail that run acrost the front of it.

About midnight there was a knock at the door. Whoever was there had come up quiet. I look out the front window. There was two men settin on the rail. I walk into the dinin room, where my two sisters was settin up in bed. "What is you done?"

"Nothin," they both say. I look out the dinin room window and there was men in the yard.

I want to tell you the honest truth that's a turrible feelin to be surrounded like that. There was one or two men at every crack that open out my house. In them days the whites would come and take people out and try to whup 'em, beat 'em to death, kill 'em. I didn't want that to happen. I had always said if the whites ever come there at me, I'm goin to make them kill me right there in front of my folks and not way off somewhere. Now I couldn't figure what to do.

I walk into my bedroom. "What is you done?" My wife was drawed up under the covers cryin and prayin.

"I ain't done nothin." When I look out the bedroom window I saw more men. I hadn't done nothin. And my little girl was too small.

I seen a Chevrolet settin out on the road.

Just walkin, walkin every which a way in my house, I didn't know what in the world to do.

"Lord have mercy," my wife cry. "Turn to the Lord."

They sure scared a fit on me. I wasn't thinkin about prayin. They kept a calling, "Ed, come on out."

"I ain't comin out there. Who is it?"

"Josh Lawson."

I thought I heard "The law." I ask him, "Who did you say that is?" My sisters both stand straight up in their double bed.

"Josh Lawson." He a bailiff. I knowed him.

"Light you a lamp."

"No, I don't need no light."

"Come on out here."

"No."

"Put your shoes on."

"All right." I set there and put my shoes on. That give me a little time to study. I had a 38 pistol and a good shotgun but

I didn't have nare cartridge and nare shell.

"Open the door."

I was shakin so bad. I crack open the door. There was a man standin with his back to the wall right next to the door. I look out right into his face. I shot the door back.

Now Josh Lawson seed I wasn't comin out unless he drug me out. "I'm lookin for McLeod," he say. "You seen McLeod?"

"Yeah, I seed him. He come by here this evenin with my brother."

"I'm comin in to search for him."

I open the door and he come on in. I had one closet. He jump backwards up in that closet. He make a show of lookin around.

"Ed, you got any good drinkin liquor?"

"No, I don't drink liquor."

They run for the car because they knowed there was too many of them for the inside of Mr. Lawson's Chevrolet. Some could hang on to the runnin boards and the last one or two would have to stick on the hood. Off they went to search the other colored people's houses.

After they left I went to my brother's house. I want him and the other colored families to know the bailiff was comin.

They had done got at Homer before they come to my house. "I was so scared I butted my head against the wall tryin to kill myself," he say.

And they had been to my brother-in-law Tommy's house. He swore he wasn't scared. "Shoot, no!" But I know he was.

McLeod's mother-in-law had a bunch of cows in the barn and he just went in there and lay down amongst them. He sneaked off and I haven't seen him since.

Me and none of my people did anythin the next day. We just laid around.

I had got to missin my Model T, so in 1932 I followed the style and made me a Hoover buggy. To do that you took the front axle of a Model T Ford and the two front wheels, and a lot of folks used the front seat with springs out of the car. It was drawn by a horse or mule and rode good with rubber tires.

Ours come in handy that summer when highway 280 was paved. We would go to town and buy groceries and my wife cooked them and I went up and down the highway in our buggy askin the workers which want to order a plate for noontime. We didn't earn much money but we sure ate good.

Later I got to work on 280 with the PWA. If you had even a bank of taters and they knowed it or if a bossman said he could take care of you, you couldn't get on.

I've seen a lot of work on highway 280. When I was a boy one of the houses we lived in was high on a hill near an old wagon road. Me and my sister Rose would set in the yard and watch the convicts gradin it with picks and shovels and mattockses and grubbin hoes. They wasn't suppose to talk with nobody but they was good at sidlin alongside someone. "Don't never come to the chain gang, boy." I didn't want to go there. When the men was whipped down in the swamp we could hear them hollerin clean back to our house.

To grade the road, men took the hills down by shovelfuls. Standin in two lines, the convicts would face each other, every man with a shovel. A mule and wagon would be driv between them lines. When the wagons got to the bottom they would be loaded.

The wagons had a bottom of two by six boards laid close so the dirt wouldn't fall through. The ends of the boards was trimmed like a handle. When the wagon got clean down the hill, men would grab a holt the ends and turn them over. The dirt fell off where it was needed. And back the men would go for another load.

Say there was a hole the chain gang captain want to fill up. He'd put his foot in the hole. "Put that dirt on my foot." The men wouldn't pick up a shovelful like they did when they was throwin dirt on the wagon, just a thin layer. They could throw that much a pretty good ways.

Shovelin and throwin and singin:

> *"Cap'n, Cap'n, has the money come?*
> *None of your business, I don't owe you none."*

They'd soon get the hole filled.

Then most of the colored couldn't look at a sheet of music and sing by notes. But the colored man had his own music in his mouth. If you can get up the spirit in a big group, it will make you feel good. The burden will lift.

After I was grown, before the tractor and the bulldozer come in, hard roads was built with mule-drawed wheelers and road scrapers. A man with a wheeler would go up a hill and get a yard of dirt or more and bring it to the road bed. Smoothin it out with the road scraper, the mules would get wide open sores as big as your hand where the collar and the backband rubbed. Men sloped the banks with pick and shovel.

The summer of 1932 when highway 280 was paved by free labor on the PWA, machinery was comin in more and more. But men still had to put their backs into the bank.

In July 1932, I got me one of the first eight-hour jobs that ever come to Abbeville in Mr. Julian Graham's sawmill. They was payin five dollars a day wages. Mr. Graham got to be the mayor of Abbeville.

The biggest thing about that sawmill was the whistle. People on the farm had always worked from sunup to dark. At the mill they'd blow the whistle for lunch and for knockin off in the evening. The people livin in town heard the whistle all the time. It got so when they went out to do farm jobs they just didn't want to work after that whistle blow.

At first everybody who could got them a job at that mill. There was the whistle. And there was another reason. Mr. Graham didn't want his hands locked up where they couldn't work. Anybody else's hands he was glad to be hard on when they come to town and done somethin called wrong. But he want his'n to get off light.

The trouble was the work at the mill was so hard you couldn't hardly make an eight-hour day. I pulled a cross saw there before the pugwood saw run by a little motor come out. Pullin that saw all day long, you had to be a man young and strong to stand it. The mosquitoes and red bugs and ticks in that swamp will eat you up.

One day when we quit for lunch I was so tired till I couldn't hardly stand up. The bossman told me, "Uncle Ed, don't set down here. Take your lunch and eat it at the well. Carry a jug and bring the rest of us back some water."

The well was about a mile and half away. The others was restin. I went on to the well, finish the day's work, and never went back.

The boss told another guy workin there to tell me not to ask for a job again 'cause he wasn't going to give me one since I had quit him.

'He can wait till I ask him for one," I say.

Finally, I got back on shares with Mr. Addison. 'We got shut of you on account of the tractor," he told me. 'And I think we got rid of the wrong man."

Other people had got to poisonin with BHC once every eight days. Mr. Addison didn't like BHC. He want to mix arsenic with molasses and mop it on the leaves, all over the cotton. If hands don't really want to, they ain't goin to do the job the way the boss wants. By the barrel he had that stuff mixed. Some of the hands would use it and some of them wouldn't. It was a tedious job and none of them thought it did much good.

This aggravate Mr. Addison. He call us together. "The boll weevil ain't just after the white man. He's after you colored too. Now I could have you usin BHC. But if I do that, it will burn you in the nose and in the throat and some of you it will make plumb sick.

"I ain't thinkin just of myself. I don't ever come out here huntin and fishin on my land. But you do. BHC poison the land and unfits it for anythin but cotton. After you use BHC you can't plant sweet potatoes or any other root crops behind cotton. The wind blow that stuff everywhere. It ruin the land for your vegetable gardens.

"The birds will eat the insects that got BHC and they'll die.

Come a big rain and the water will run off the fields into the fish ponds and kill the fish.

"People have different ways to dodge the boll weevils. This is the way I want to do it. I want you to help me."

After that some of them did a little better but not much.

That year I was the only hand Mr. Addison had to come out of debt and make money. I did it by usin my idea as to what to do and not the idea of Mr. Huey Lindley, the new overseer, who claim the only way to make a crop was to go ahead and plow, wet or dry. The cotton come up good but in June it rain almost every day and kept the ground boggy wet.

The other hands was workin for wages. Mr. Lindley had them sloshin around in the wet. He come to me. "Go ahead. The others are plowin."

I knowed not to work in the mud 'cause if you do, your land will get hard and clodded and your crop won't grow. So I went rabbit huntin and fishin, waitin for my farm to dry off. Whenever I seed Mr. Lindley peepin around my place I'd get me somethin to do. Maybe I'd hoe a few bushes or I'd take me my Dixie turnin plow and bar off some corn comin up in the Bermuda grass, or fool around with the plow like I was repairin it.

Mr. Lindley was in the habit of comin around about once a week. One time I was settin under a tree. "You still layin around the house?" The next time he brung a man with him. "Ed, if you ain't goin to work your crop, I got another man that will."

"I'll work it," I told him. I wait two more days; my crop good and dry. Then I get out early with a scrape and scooter and stayed late. I really got my crop cleaned out.

The best part was that on fifteen acres I made eleven bales of cotton behind one mule. I come out of debt and cleared one hundred and sixty dollars. Mr. Lindley didn't do so good. Sun and drought come and made the ground hard and scald the crop. Most of the men under Mr. Lindley that year made one or two bales of cotton. Three was the limit. And on Mr. Addison's one hundred–acre tractor farm Mr. Lindley made fifteen bales of cotton.

Mr. Addison turnt him off. "Ed, I'm proud to know you. If Mr. Lindley had done as good as you, I'd be a lot better off."

"Yes, sir," I say, "you really need a good overseer." Mr. Jackson and Mr. Lindley wasn't neither one no count. I was a good farmer and I knowed how to get other people to really put out. I would have made a better overseer than Mr. Addison ever had.

He called hisself a good man. And other people, colored and white, called Colonel Addison a good man. But bein white, he was handicapped to where he couldn't see the overseer in me.

I could really farm and Mr. Addison knew it. By rights I was due to make somethin. "Mr. Addison," I say, "I want to farm on standin rent." That's the deal a tenant makes to pay so much rent an acre for the use of the land. The owner don't get nothin else. But rentin can be tough too. If you have a family they mouths never close except over food. Until you make the crop you'll more than likely need furnish money. The boss will get his 10 per cent interest.

If you don't pay your rent, the landlord can level on you and take your stock up to what you owe him. He can sell anythin you got.

Several ways to farm have been figured out to be justice if the boss and the tenant both do right. There's share croppin, or rentin, or thirds, or fourths. But it's hard to find a boss or a tenant who really want to be fair to the other.

"Well, go to it, Ed," Mr. Addison tell me when I ask about standin rent.

Mr. Addison was a sure enough lawyer. I've heard it said that if he was on the other side, you was a gonner. But he didn't know nothin about farmin. He let us pay him five dollars an acre rent on land we planted in cotton and three dollars an acre for land in corn and velvet beans. That was a little too cheap.

I made an extra good crop that year and bought me a Model T Ford for seventy-five dollars cash. Mr. Addison told me I had got the big end of the stick and that for the next crop we was going to be on shares.

Me and my brother-in-law, Tom Sparrow, figure the real reason Mr. Addison change our standing rent deal back to shares was that we sold our cotton in Rochelle for the market price. When you rentin you supposed to get the privilege to sell to anyone you want, and to gin your cotton anywhere you can get the best deal.

But Mr. Addison didn't like it that way. He want to buy cotton from his renters under the market price and to sell it in Savannah, Georgia. That way he got his lick at it. "I was expectin you to bring cotton to me. You and Sparrow took it to Rochelle."

So my rentin come to an end after just one year. If I had had my rathers I would have been on standin rent. But I couldn't complain. I was back on shares and I did get half. Mr. Addison had a divided crib to put the corn in, my half on one side and his half on the other. All around me there was tenants that didn't fare as good as me.

12 From small on up, our daughter Lottie was
the biggest parents' pet I ever knowed in my life. One time I told
my wife, "Time you get that baby dressed there ain't goin to be
no ribbons left nowhere in the world."

My wife would hold up our girl even before she start to talk
and declare, "Ain't that the *smartest* baby," and laugh and go
on.

"That a smart girl," her teacher say when she went to
school. And happy. Just a movin all the time. She never walk
if she could skip. And she like to run. "I'm goin to run you down
a gopher hole," I'd say when I went to catch her.

One day me and my wife got to talkin with Mattie Mae Irwin
in town. She had a new baby.

"That a pretty baby," I tell her. "How about givin him to
me?"

"You can have him. But wait till in the mornin. I'm goin to
carry him home and get his clothes."

"Is you foolin?"

"No, I ain't foolin."

"I'll meet you in front of the post office at nine o'clock
tomorrow mornin."

"Well, you can sure look to see me there."

I had been wantin a boy for the longest.

My wife say, "You know she ain't goin to give that baby
away. You crazy. She just teasin."

But I knowed and my wife knowed Mattie Mae Irwin had
done give away three babies, all she to have, like that. I argued
for gettin him. My wife got mad. "What I want a baby for? I
don't want no baby. I want to school the one I got."

I didn't go get him. Mattie Mae give him away and for a long time whenever I seed him I wished he was mine.

Up till Lottie got to be almost courtin size she growed up just as easy. She was tall and large. I think that what made her call herself courtin so soon. That was the only daughter I had and, quite natural, I want to see at her the best I could.

The town just had two streets. When we went there she'd go down on the other corner and stay off from around me. When she'd look up I wouldn't be right at her. But I'd be standin where I could see her.

"Daddy, ain't you watchin me?"

"No, what I'm watchin you for?"

I was watchin all right. I want her to go to school and my wife even want her to finish high school. The boys had started comin. So I tell Lottie, "I'm gonna get you a radio to have in the livin room." I wasn't studyin about her gettin married.

My wife caught Miss Babe Blakeley tellin Lottie, "I don't care what your daddy buy. That radio won't be yourn; it'll still be his'n. Go get a house of your own."

The lady Babe Blakeley cook for, Miss Martha Tucker, liked to know who was courtin each other, colored or white. Babe Blakeley kept Miss Martha up with what was goin on amongst the colored.

In a dream my wife seed Miss Martha and Babe Blakeley fanning a spark with the fans like they had at the white folks' church. They made a big fire. Then all at once it just went out.

Lottie got in with Luther Newman 'cause he was workin for wages for Mr. Sargent Pike and whenever anyone come from the Pike place to the road they had to go through my field. Luther was all right, I guess, but I didn't know nothin about his folks and Lottie didn't either. I was wantin her to marry someone I knowed.

Just after they married in the courthouse at Abbeville one Saturday evenin the father of another boy who courted Lottie pass there. "Your daughter must have had to marry that boy."

"No," I say, "she didn't have to marry nobody."

Talk about a throwed-away crowd, we felt like one. That

night me and my wife couldn't hardly go home. I ask her, "Mae, you want me to buy you a dress?"

"No, I don't want no dress. What I want a dress for?"

We got in our Hoover buggy and went on home. Look like we was just missin somethin. Finally, we got over it.

Buddie and Emma Lou was born. Lottie's husband never would agree to have them with him. He didn't seem to like chillen, not too long at the time. I figure it might have been 'cause he was so young. When Lottie plowed and chopped cotton for Mr. Sargent Pike she lef the kids with us. Takin care of them was a lot for my wife to do.

The way Lottie and her husband kept fussin and fightin worry my wife. They'd go after each other on the street. Anywhere.

Luther went to the army and they sent him to Japan, where he stayed about two years. He had a 32 Smith and Wesson that he lef with me. "If I don't get back, you have it. If I get back, I want it." The first thing he ask for when he come back in the house was that pistol. I give it to him.

After he stay around the house a week or two he got a job workin in a store in Orlando, Florida. Him and Lottie lef the chillen with us and went down there.

One evenin about sundown here come Scott Temple. He work on the railroad but he was at Mr. Sapp's store when the telephone call from Florida come there for me. He brought me the message: Come, and come at once. Lottie kilt her husband.

It took me and Willie Mae a while to get ready. I borrowed money from Mr. Addison and from Mr. Emory Oakes and I had some myself. The white folks knowed I hadn't never been off nowhere. They told me how to do it. "Ed, when you go down there, get in with a preacher. Ask him what lawyer to get."

This white person say, "Anythin I can do to help you, let me know." That one give me a little change. When he seed me gettin on the bus Mr. Joe Lynn give me a pack of cigarettes. He was the one wouldn't light the cigar he kept in his mouth, and wouldn't give out no Christmas less'n you ask him.

All the way to Orlando my wife named every colored person she had ever heard of who was let off for killin another colored. It hadn't been long before that Hal Halston, a colored boy in our settlement, had shot and killed another colored boy who come there from Florida to visit his parents. After shootin him Hal took the boy to the doctor. One night in jail was what Hal got. He claim the boy had been prankin with a gun.

On back further the white folks would stand up for you if they had you tagged for one who minded them. If the boss had money, there wouldn't be nothin he couldn't take care of if he want to. More'n likely he'd say, "Go on home. I'll see at it."

Travelin, I couldn't sleep, Willie Mae neither. I kept studyin how to get a preacher, how to get a lawyer, how to get my daughter off.

Time I got to Orlando I went to see Lottie. The sheriff didn't let me go up in the jail to see her. He brought her down to see was I her daddy. She was cryin when she come down. "I didn't mean to do it."

"I didn't come to dog you. I come to help you."

My sister Julie Mae was livin in Orlando. She carry my wife and me to see the place where Lottie and Luther had boarded. Their landlady ask us to come in and we set there and listened.

"Lottie would get mad and would speak things. Luther would try to shame her out of them. Lottie told me they had done parted. 'If you all done parted, Lottie,' I say, 'I don't want no trouble in my house. You know you man and wife. So he may come here and raise sand.'

" 'Nobody know Luther but me,' Lottie say. She would talk about how mean he was. 'I just can't go back to him.'

"She show me some pictures of they chillen. 'Ain't they the cutest little things you ever seed?' The little girl was just like her, the little boy was just like him.

"Saturday evenin he come. I say, 'I thought you gone, Luther.'

" 'No'm.'

"They loved around here. Lottie set in his lap all Saturday

evenin, and Sunday we all three went to church together. Sunday after church they went to they room. I was ready to go back to church Sunday evenin when she come out. 'You done dressed and goin to walk out and leave me here.' She ask me did I have any perfume.

" 'No, I don't have no perfume because I hardly ever use it.'

" 'I'm goin back in the room and talk to my husband.' I heard her say, 'Luther, what the matter? What wrong with you?'

"By him speakin so low I couldn't understand him. But I heard somethin, seem like somethin hit—boompf! I was settin by the radio rockin. I thought it was outdoors.

"Lottie come flyin out the room. She had a black pistol—but the handle was shiny—wavin it every way, this way, that way, swingin her arm around. She was hollerin, 'Lord, I done kilt my husband. I done shot Luther.'

" 'Oh, Lottie.'

" 'If you don't believe it, go look. Lord, have mercy! I wouldn't have did it for nothin!'

"When she got to the door she drop the gun on a bag I had on the porch. When I walk in they room I saw him settin there in the chair. One of his feets was stretched way out. He had his head bowed, the blood runnin. His mouth was open. I couldn't stand it. I went out the house. Until the policemen come I didn't pick up the gun and I didn't let nobody pick it up. If Lottie hadn't run out and hollered, she could have run off, I reckon. 'Cause I wasn't payin no 'tention. That noise didn't sound like a gun to me."

Now I ask my sister to carry me to her preacher. That was a nice old preacher. He set there and he talk and he talk to me and my wife. "Lawyer Sharp is the best lawyer we got in this town. If you was able to get him, I know your daughter would come clear."

"You reckon? Well, that's the one I want."

My sister carry me to his office. He was a short, stuffy-built man. I explain myself.

"It will take five hundred dollars to carry this through."

"How would I have to pay it?"

"I want one hundred and fifty of it down, and whenever she's clear, you'll have to give me the other."

"I wonder would you know where the nearest rest room for colored at?"

"About four blocks straight down the street at the court-house." I goes there. Next to my skin I had me a money belt around my waist. Back I goes to Lawyer Sharp's office and give him three hundred dollars, two times what he ask for. He give me his card and tell me, "I'll be too glad to help you."

"Well, I hired him," I tell my wife.

When the colored people found out I had Lawyer Sharp, they come round. "Man, you got the best lawyer. Your daughter ain't goin nowhere."

"Well, that's my daughter, and if I had money, I couldn't enjoy it and know I could have got her out."

I stay around there till after the inquest. That's the trial to bind you over to the big court or let you go. It was then my wife went to moanin. Moanin and moanin out loud.

At the commitment trial a letter Luther had wrote was read: "Lottie, I did want you. But I don't now 'cause you done me so bad till I am sad."

Lottie's landlady was asked did Lottie and Luther have any trouble the night before the shootin and she say, "No, sir. They didn't. Both of them act mighty nice."

"Very lovin?"

"Yes, sir. And they went to church with me Sunday mornin."

A man ownin a pawnshop say, "Luther pawned his gun three times. The last time he took it out was April eleventh, nineteen forty-six." That was the day before the shootin.

When he went to hand the gun back to the officer—he was named Greeley—the pawnbroker just hand it to him, like he was handin on somethin not much account. But I notice when Officer Greely taken it he sort of pet it and rub the pearl handle like it was really somethin.

He talk about the killin. "Some white man come up and said he heard a woman screamin down back of a buildin toward Jackson Street. Officer Phillips and I went to investigate. There was quite a big crowd gatherin.

"This woman came to me out of the crowd and informs me she had just killed her husband and to do somethin with her, and she went further to state she wouldn't have done it for anythin in the world. They was playin cowboy with a pistol when it happened, that he told her the gun wasn't loaded, that he first drew it on her, then gave it to her and told her to pull it on him."

Then they call Officer Phillips and he told how pieces of Luther's brain lay on his leg. "We immediately taken the woman to the station. We taken her down and lock her up. She ask us to let her know as quick as we could if he was dead.

"She was awfully hysterical for a while. She said ever since he got back that he had a habit of twirlin that gun on his finger and snappin it, playin with it, and he was learnin her how to do it.

"When she killed him the gun was held almost against the skin. She told us he had been actin awful peculiar ever since he come back from overseas. Always talkin about dyin."

A man read out the coroner's verdict: "We the jury find that Luther Mack Newman come to his death April eleventh by gunshot wound by hand of Lottie Newman and we recommend she be held for manslaughter. So say we all of us."

My wife went to moanin and cryin. "Just wait a minute," I tell her.

I go to the lawyer. "Look a here, I thought you was goin to get my daughter to come clear."

"I like to got her clear but there wasn't no snap bullet in the gun. Some of the jury just wasn't satisfied. Come to my office." I goes there. "I'll sure fix it up if you let me have the pistol to give to Officer Greeley when the trial come up. When you're fixin for someone to come clear you really need the police to help you. If you wouldn't mind him havin the gun, I'd appreciate it."

"Yeah, you can have the pistol, I don't want it." So I reckon he give Officer Greeley the pistol.

"You can just go back home and rest because I'm goin to send your daughter to you." He told me he could law in every state of the Union. "I could come to Georgia and help you."

"When you get her out I'll send you the other money."

"All right."

I was goin to get Lottie out on bond. But they run the bond way up higher than I could stand. Lawyer Sharp advise, "Just let her stay in there. It ain't goin to hurt her. She goin to be took good care of. You'll know where she at."

"Well, you right."

That night just before supper here come a Red Cross lady to the place me and my wife was stayin. "You all can go home. You all done everythin you can."

We got on the bus that night.

First thing I did when I got home was to scrape up the rest of the money. I was ready. I didn't figure we had to go back but my wife wanted to be with Lottie. We found out when the trial was and I sent my wife back.

At the trial Officer Greeley testify that pictures of white women was found on the body of Luther Newman. To my knowin and to Lottie's knowin Luther had never had nothin to do with no white woman. But Lottie come home clear and that's what I was after.

Now I halfway wish I had let her make a little time. If I could have knowed she'd get about twelve months . . . somethin like that have helped chillen sometimes. You keep payin them out, payin them out. That was the first thing I ever had to pay her out.

A lady ask me once, "Who did you get to help you get your daughter out?" Her daughter had kilt a man.

"What you mean?"

"You didn't get no root worker? Nobody to help you?"

"No. The way I got her out was with money."

Comin back on the bus my wife say, "Lottie, Babe Blakeley the one got you to marry Luther."

"Miss Babe oughta been kilt."

Time Lottie got off the bus she say, "I got a baby comin." My wife had gone to moanin. Moanin, moanin. I couldn't stop her. She couldn't stop herself.

About six months after her daddy died Lola was born. "Jest look at her," my wife say. "She's just a darin us not to love her." We loved her all right. You love all your chillen but it sort of look like to me Lola was smarter than the others. She was a right cute child.

Lola and Buddie and Emma Lou didn't call me Grand-daddy. Daddy was how they call me. Me and my wife looked after them the best we know how. Lottie married Scott Temple and leave the three chillen with us when her and him went to New York.

One day we was in town. Lola hadn't been walkin long. She runned out in the street. A farmer named Dan Otis was comin along in his car and he knock her down and she went under the car, but he didn't run over her.

My heart was knockin so when I went out in the street and pick her up I couldn't hardly walk to the curb. I set down there and it seem like it took me the longest to get my strength back to where I could stand up. Me and my wife took her to the doctor. There wasn't nothin wrong no more than we was all scared.

I thought Dan Otis should have stopped. He didn't. But he come to me afterwards and said the reason he didn't stop was because he had a load of moonshine in his car. "Look a here," he ask, "don't you want to bring your cane to my mill?" I took it there and after he grind the cane he cook the juice in his evaporator and make syrup. He didn't charge me nothin.

13   Until recent years I was afraid of hants. And my wife was very scared of them, a heap more than me.

Back when my wife was small the county was wet. Comin home from town in the wagon Saturday night if anythin got at the mule Willie Mae's ma would figure it was a ghost. She'd take some whiskey and pour it out on the road so the ghost would suck it up and quit botherin the mule.

When a mule's tail got tied up in knots Willie Mae's mother would claim a witch been ridin him. My wife had heard that from small on up. She never would work a mule like that.

One time Willie Mae told our pastor, "The first time I ever member seein a hant, me and my brother was layin in front of the fire. I had my feets toward the fire and my head back the other way. We had a switch we had been playin with. Sleep come over me and when I woke up my head was layin in a baby's lap. The baby didn't have no arms. 'Look a there,' I told my brother. 'Look a there.'

"The baby had on a napkin and a dress with embroidery trimmin. I grabbed the switch and took after the baby with it. Right on in the fire the baby went. I slap my hand over my eyes. We went outdoors and alarm up the settlement hollerin."

Our pastor say, "That was your imagination."

"If it was," Willie Mae say, "it was the purest imagination I ever seed in my life."

Sometimes when she talk about that I would tell how before we was married I went one evening to see a friend. Right in between John's house and mine was an old house well knowed to be hanted. On nights when the moon was shinin I didn' much like to do it but I'd walk right by it. But one dark night when

I stayed late, I told John, "I ain't goin by that hanted house. I'm goin from here way behind it right acrost the swamp home."

Then in the country people used lighterwood splinters for torches. John give me some and I set out with a light.

"Go ahead," he say. "I'm goin to sort of watch over you."

I was totin my light lookin down. And honestly, truly, I went from his house straight to the middle of the swamp and right to the back door of the old house I didn't want to go by. I look down and there was the steps and I was about to walk right up them. I throwed my light down and stomp it out, walk on around the house and went down the road home.

Later John say, "I thought you wasn't goin by that house. It look to me like you went right to it."

"I reckon the Lord had me come up the back of that house to show me there wasn't no hants to bother me."

I didn't believe in unseen things and yet I did. I've seed many things that if it wasn't a hant, I couldn't make out what else it was. When I was a boy there was no one I knowed of didn't believe in them. I knowed one old man that wasn't afraid of them. "Look, Ed, there's an old ghost." Sometimes I couldn't see nothin, sometimes I'd see a white spot. And then I'd go to chillin and sweatin.

For a while back when we all work for Mr. Jim McHenry, me and my wife and her brother Tommy and his wife all slept in the same room. Tommy and his wife was in they bed on that side of the room and me and my wife in ourn over here. We wasn't asleep and hadn't been to sleep. Somethin was knockin the nail keg just as plain. It was full of buck, the stuff we had to make beer with, and we hadn't been long put it in the shed.

"Do you hear that?" Tommy ask.

We laid there and listen at it. I say, "Let's go in there and see what it is."

I step out of my bed and walk on by his. He had on a long nightshirt. I was walkin behind. I call myself lettin him lead.

When I got in the kitchen I couldn't see him no more.

I call, "Hey, Tommy!"

"Hey!" he say. And he was in his bed.

"You ain't been out the bed?"

"No."

I flew back out that kitchen and got back in the bed.

I don't know whether my eyes could have fooled me that bad or not. It look like to me there was a man walkin ahead of me just as sure as day.

There was strange things there at Mr. McHenry's. In the evenin we would sit on the porch. A dog would jump over the fence and go right after somethin. Barkin and bitin and scratchin just like he attackin somebody. "What he after?" my wife ask.

The house we was in wasn't sealed in no way. Somethin would go in and look like we could hear it eat. We'd lay in bed and listen at it. My wife kept a punchin me. "Ed, you hear that?"

I yell out, "YES, I HEAR IT."

After that it look like they didn't bother us so much.

One night—it was right in the summertime and fair as a lily —the moon was shinin and I was settin in the window. My wife was gettin our supper ready. I heard a man come up to the window like he was so tired. Sighin and sighin. So tired. We look for the man. And look and look. And I ain't never seed nobody yet.

My wife was one to go by dreams. Once she found a big gopher. She cook it and we all eat it for dinner. She laid down and went to sleep. A gopher crawl right up to her, bow up on his legs, and say, "You got to lay down and die just like I did."

After that dream my wife say, "I ain't never goin to eat no more gophers."

When my wife took sick Dr. Acton claim it was because she believe too much in root workers and unseen things. But I don't hardly think it was that. I have knowed many people that believe in unseen things that didn't get sick.

I really think it because so many things worried my wife. There was the trouble we had collectin the insurance for the grandchillen. When our daughter Lottie's husband, Luther Newman, went into the army he took out a ten thousand dollar policy and make it to his chillen, Buddie and Emma Lou. About three or four days before the insurance went dead he got killed.

The man that come to pay off the policy told my wife he'd give it all to her but that it wouldn't do for her to have that much money, her being colored. Other people say it because she not really in her right mind.

So he had the county ordinary make Mr. Baxter Upshaw the guardian. Nare time did the chillen get a check from the government. They got Mr. Upshaw's personal check. He claim ten dollars a month was as much as the government would allow him to pay for each child.

"I got to feed, house, clothe, and school them. Ten dollars a month is not enough. I won't take that," I told Mr. Upshaw.

One white fellow told me, "I don't blame you, Ed. I wouldn't let him give it out that way, but don't tell him I said nothin about it." Another claim it wasn't right, the chillen wasn't gettin enough of it. My wife want to be guardian to avoid all them charges. I was cut out account I couldn't read and write.

Mr. Upshaw swear it wasn't nothin to him but he wouldn't give it up. He kept right on gettin his lick at it.

Somethin happen that worry my wife. It would worry anybody.

One Sunday me and my wife decide we want to go fishin. We hitch up the mules to our Hoover buggy and we leave the three grandchillen at home. Time we leave them kids go to cookin. My wife had cooked dinner already, so the stove already hot.

When Lola poured in some kerosene it must have exploded on her. Over half her skin was burnt off her. She was just like raw meat.

When we come back the other chillen had wrapped her in a blanket and taken her down the road to wait for us. If we had sent her to the hospital she might have got better. But she was burnt so bad till I wanted to keep her at home to see do she have good attention.

I had Dr. Durham to look at Lola and he tell me, "There ain't much you can do for this chile. She done lost too much skin."

Mrs. King—Ma King was what the colored call her behind her back—had the job of bossin the welfare. She heard about our trouble and come to my house.

If anyone didn't have a husband and was kind of old and just had a little speck of somethin, she'd tell 'em, "I'll put you on welfare, you trade with me." She knowed exactly what everybody was gettin and she'd have the account up to that at her store.

The last time I had seed Ma King was one day I had some hands pickin cotton. At noon they want some cold drinks and knick knacks. I had them get on the truck and we went to Mrs. King's store. I got me a can of pork and beans and some salt crackers. She charge me twenty cents for the beans.

Comin back, one of them workin with me say, "Good gracious, them things ain't but ten cents."

Mrs. King look at Lola and say she know a doctor that live acrost the river at Milam, Georgia. "I know he can do you good. He the one I use." She goes for him and bring him back and he charge twenty dollars. Mrs. King bought the salve the doctor want us to use. "It's a special mixture," she say. "That's why it cost ten dollars."

The expenses was carryin me downhill so fast till I tell Mrs. King not to bring the doctor back no more. I tell my wife, "Let's you and me go with Ma King and find out where she gettin that medicine." She carry us to the drugstore the doctor own in Milam.

Comin on back home, I want somethin cold like a popsicle. When we got to Ryan I give Mrs. King fifteen cents to get me one, her one, and my wife one. Popsicles have got two rolls of frozen ice on two sticks. In place of buyin three when she went in the drugstore Mrs. King bought two. She eat half of one. Then she broke the other popsicle in half.

She come out to the car and give me one half and my wife the other. And she eat the last part of the one she start eatin in the store. That way she made a nickel. When Mrs. King wasn't lookin, my wife make a big face at her and stick out her tongue.

The next time the baby need salve me and my wife went to where Mrs. King had carried us. Two dollars and fifty cents was what we paid for it.

My wife know a colored fellow that work in the drugstore. He say Ma King was dopin and the doctor all the time fussin at her and threatenin not to give her no more shots unless she get him up some money. I think that how come my bill so high.

We had Lola under a big mosquito net and we kept puttin salve on the burnt part. She got pneumonia.

"I'm goin to die. I'm goin to leave you. I want you to pray."

"You gonna stay with granddaddy. You ain't goin to die."

"Yeah, I'm goin to die. And I always want you to pray. And be good."

"All right. I'm goin to be good."

I was settin there and she would doze and wake, doze and wake. Somethin make a noise outside the house and she just wake up and look and then died.

That a pretty hurtin thing. Pretty hurtin.

We buried her at Piney Grove Baptist Church. Lola would never have to grow old, the preacher say, we would always think of her as a beautiful little girl. "What make him think I don't want Lola to grow old?" my wife ask. "I sure didn't want her to die young."

Not long after that my wife dream of seein Lola about sixteen. " 'Here what I would have looked like if I'd a stayed.' "

"That was a beautiful girl," my wife say.

Dr. Durham was in our settlement one evenin and he come
by and set on my porch awhile. I tell him about Lola wantin me
to pray and be good. "I try to be the best I can but I ain't all
that good. I reckon I ain't all that bad either."

"That's right, Ed, you don't want to be too good. Don't be
so good the Lord will covet you. Don't be bad enough the devil
will get you. Be sort of 'twixt and between, sort of half good and
half bad, so don't nare one of them want you. You'll live a long
time."

One day when I was workin in the field I kept a thinkin
about Lola. Finally I just give up and brung my mule to the
house. My friend John Kemp come by and we goes to town. We
was settin on the curb near the drugstore.

I was tellin him how Lola come in my mind very often. It
seem like since she pass nothin right. I hadn't never paid the
courthouse clock no mind. It wouldn't keep time by no com-
mand. Here lately it had been botherin me. Most everybody
knowed how to keep time by it. Every time it struck we'd go to
addin seventeen minutes and that'd give us the time.

We was better off in Abbeville than in Tifton, where there
is no clock on the courthouse. People claim when it was built
they didn't put a clock there because then the niggers could tell
time by it.

Lola wasn't no big child, she had just started goin to school,
but she had such good sense.

When John and me talkin, I see a little blonde, curly-headed
girl driv by a lady in a car. They come by us and the girl put
her fingers in a V and spit towards me.

"Well, look a there," John Kemp say.

The lady haul the girl around the block and slow down in
front of us for her to spit again. And another time. And another.

As God is my secret judge, it come to my mind to kill that
woman. She was mean-hearted and teachin that chile to be
hateful. I didn't want her to live.

John Kemp say, "It's best we hit the road." We got in his
car and left.

After Lola died my wife went back to readin the Bible. And she would borrow books from the colored school. That bother her as much as readin the Bible. "It don't say the colored this and the whites that. It say the citizens of the United States. The colored is citizens. We pay taxes. Our money good. Shoot!" The library in Abbeville was for whites. My wife didn't like that. "I ain't goin to ruin them books."

Her mother died. Willie Mae and her sisters and Emmett went lookin at caskets. Everyone was goin to pay his part in the funeral. I tell them, "I got it ready."

Mrs. Sparrow was layin there embalmed. I ask my wife, "What the matter they don't bury your mother?"

"I don't think they got no money."

I had five hundred dollars buried in my cow stable—the first time I ever had that much money I didn't owe somebody. I just count out the whole amount they was needin for the funeral and give it to them.

We was keepin the grand-chillen even after Lottie married Scott Temple. The first we knowed of them partin was when Lottie come home from New York one fall and brung the three kids her and Scott had and Jimmy with her. He was a short, brown-skinned fellow with a fat, round face.

Jimmy was raised in New York City. About one hundred or one hundred and fifty pounds was what he pick when he really put out. But when Lottie went to pickin, he want her to rush. My wife spoke about it. "Jimmy, if you wants any more cotton picked, go pick it yourself."

I was busy pickin cotton and I wasn't payin much attention 'cause they say they was married. But my wife was. She was pretty strict on that and at the time I was too. "I don't think they married," she say. "Where they license?"

My wife kept doggin me—so I want to know was they married.

"Yeah, our license in the trunk."

It never did come. I ask them straight about it.

Lottie say, "We not married but we love one another."

"That ain't worth nothin." Buddie was about seventeen. "Crank up that truck, Buddie." I got my rifle. I told Jimmy, "You get on that truck."

He didn't want to do it. "You all sure breakin up two people that love one another," he say.

"I ain't breakin up nothin." I carried him to Abbeville. "Four corners of that road there. This one goes to Hawkinsville, that one goes to Fitzgerald, that one to Ryan, but you don't want to go back this way to Rochelle 'cause I'm back there."

He went to Hawkinsville. When me and Eddie Lee come back home we met Lottie walkin. "Don't bring him back," I tell her.

They got in jail fightin out in the streets. Lottie call me and I went and got her out of jail. He was standin back in another cell. "Daddy, what you gonna do about me?" he ask.

"Not a thing."

Finally somebody got him out. Lottie went on with him. "She's goin to hang with you," I say.

After a while she got tired of him and put him outdoors.

Then she run the café but while she was tryin to keep down one fight people would steal money out the piccalo. She give that up.

Gardner was the next fellow she taken up with and by him she got four chillen.

Lottie had to work. It was mostly anythin she could get to do. My wife try to look after the grandchillen. It was too much.

14 Me and my wife's mother, Mrs. Sally Sparrow, always got on pretty good. But when Dr. Acton say my wife had lost her mind and ought to go to the hospital, her ma claim, "There ain't nothin about Willie Mae to cause her to go to the hospital 'cept you done tricked her. You ain't put none of her hair in runnin water, is you? 'Cause that'll sure drive anybody crazy."

"Ed, I'm goin to tell you the truth," Dr. Acton say, "they claim our mental hospital is the worst in the United States, 'cept for the one they got in Mississippi. But it's the only place you can send your wife and she'll be better off there than at home."

The day he told me that I had been in the field with some chillen pickin cotton. My wife come out there holdin a butcher knife behind her back.

I tell them, "Don't pay her no 'tention."

"Yeah," one of them say, "but I'm afraid she might hurt me with that knife."

The evenin before, my wife had set on the porch watchin me. Once I raise my arm and point the chillen to where I had set the water bucket. My wife claim I was tryin to get the rest of them to leave the field and go in the woods so I could court this girl about fifteen. She was a girl that was always talkin to me about my grandson. She liked him.

When my wife come to the field I say, "You can ask them. I ain't done nothin to none of them."

"I'm goin to tell Miss Joe Phillips"—she was the chillen's grandma—"you ain't fitten to hire no chillen."

"Go tell her whatever you damn please." She kept standin there. "Go to the house, I'll be in there directly."

When I goes in from work she had the three youngest grandchillen on one side of the fireplace covered up with a blanket. She was between them and me, tryin to keep them away from me. I was always one to devil the chillen and to get the boys down and play with them.

She didn't want me to touch them. It sort of vexed me but I didn't say nothin. She get in the bed and raise a curious fuss. I goes back there. Many times, when she come sick like women do, she'd tell me to get some kerosene and rub it up and down her back and on the bottom of her feets. She'd purr like a cat. I did that now.

But she didn't favor herself. I thought the blood had went to her head. She was cold and shakin and went to havin a hard chill. It seem like she passed out. I rub under the bottom of her feet and she come to. "What are you tryin to do, trick me?"

"No," I say, "I'm tryin to do you some good."

She cuss me out. And my ma. And went to sayin all kinds of things she had never said before. Then she pass out again. I run and got a neighbor to come stay till I could find Dr. Acton.

The reason we was alone in the house was my wife had run off our boarder. We had most always had a schoolteacher to stay with us. But everytime I'd go off rabbit huntin or to work for someone else my wife thought I was runnin after the teacher. After my wife claim I drunk wine with the teacher I told her, "You better see can you find another place to live."

I knowed then there was somethin or 'nother wrong.

Dr. Acton come and my wife tell him, "I ain't takin no medicine. You ain't goin to trick me." She quieted off but she wouldn't take the medicine. Dr. Acton set there half an hour or more talkin to her. Then he told me to come outside.

Walkin to his car, he ask, "Has Willie Mae ever done this before?"

"No, but it has got to where I just can't satisfy her. Look like she done got mean. Anythin I say she answer, 'That a lie.' "

Dr. Acton stop and stood there awhile. He got out his pipe, fill it, and lit it, and he look straight at me. "Ed, your wife has lost her mind. I don't know whether you got any money but the only thing will do her any good is to go to the state hospital at Milledgeville. They got treatments up there to bring her back to her mind."

When I went back in the house Willie Mae was layin there asleep. I want to talk to her about how she had lost her mind but I knowed I couldn't do that so I laid down but I couldn't sleep.

Wide awake. I went way back there to when me and Willie Mae courted and come right on up to now. Until she took sick we got along pretty good most of the time. I'd say like two peas in a hull.

We had fights and we had our ups and downs but we didn't let it amount to much. Almost always we managed to have plenty to eat. If either of us had a dime the other could spend it. Finally we got up where we had somethin of our own. If they want me to sell them somethin, near about all the white folks that knowed me would say, "Go ask your wife," 'cause they knew that's what I'd do.

Either she worked washin and ironin or cookin for wages— even when I first got her she was a pretty good cook—or she worked farmin. She could make clothes and can and preserve. The cakes she baked was just naturally better than any I ever eat since. She would take a fork and make holes in the top and when she ice it that gracious goodness would sink all down through it.

We would plow side by side and hoe cotton and corn side by side. And she really enjoyed it. I used to tell her, "Me and you goin to die together out in the field settin alongside a stump."

She could hitch up a mule and drive one as good as anybody. I have had people to tell me she could plow better than I could. Until our daughter got up big enough to help me out some my wife done all my readin and writin and seed at our business. No white folks I knowed of ever kicked on her bookkeepin.

She liked to go to church and to fix dinner for the preacher.

After my daughter got in trouble my wife went to moanin

and prayin out loud. She took to readin the Bible a lot. Readin in the Revelations will scare anybody. I'd tell her, "It'll make anyone uneasy to set and read the Bible all the time." But she'd do it. If the Bible right, ain't many people goin to Heaven.

I reckon she got to worryin about her soul.

That was the way I spent the night, thinkin about her. The next mornin I get up early and goes to Rochelle to see her mother, Mrs. Sparrow.

"You done conjured her," my mother-in-law say. "That about what happened. Ain't no use sendin Willie Mae away. I'm goin to bring her back to her mind. I'll get somebody stronger with the Lord than you is to take off the spell."

"I ain't tricked nobody. First place, I don't know how."

"Won't be long till I find out if you trick her," Mrs. Sparrow say. "I'm goin to carry her to Aunt Jane."

Goin to root workers was the very opposite to what Dr. Acton told me to do. But I had to get my wife's family to sign the papers so I could carry her to the asylum.

"You was runnin all over to root workers when you lost your hog," Maureen, my wife's sister say. "Look like you'd believe in them now."

It was true I had went to plenty of root workers, white and colored, and hauled people to them in my car. None of it will work if you don't believe in it. My wife believe in root workers but I didn't never want to believe in them too much because then they can handle you.

When I driv my wife and her ma to Aunt Jane's she was out in the yard. The others got out the car and I tell them I ain't comin in. "Look at him," Aunt Jane say. "He don't believe in hisself and nobody else neither."

I went on in. It didn't seem like Aunt Jane knowed me and my wife. We had been to her several years before 'cause my wife had wanted me to ask about a sow I caught in the swamp that was about to come in with pigs. Nobody hadn't seen her in around three weeks. I didn't have but this one hog at the time so I was sort of desperate.

Aunt Jane say, "Some white people got your hog fastened up in a new barn." Sure enough some white people had built one just about a mile back of my house. Aunt Jane give me some spices and cinnamon bark to chew while I was talkin to them. "Spit towards them but don't let them see you do it. That will make them tell what you want to know."

Me and my friend Will Olesby get up Sunday mornin and goes hog huntin over to the white people's place. Will ask, "You mind if I step in your beautiful new barn and look around?"

"Why, just help yourself," the white man say. I chewed that cinnamon till my mouth sore. While he wasn't lookin I spit. Then I ask is he seed my hog. "No," he say.

Will tell me, "The barn is full of hogs but yourn ain't in there. I really think Aunt Jane better for white people than she is for colored. You ought to ask Uncle Tom."

He the one found my hog, "Go about two miles from your house north by an oak tree," Uncle Tom say. "You'll find your hog with a nice litter of pigs."

When I got back home I driv up under the shelter and the first thing I seed when I got down from the car was the hog's tracks where she had went acrost the plowed dirt. She had walked from her bed at the head of the swamp straight to the shelter and back to her bed. There I found her. She had good use of herself and she had nine little pigs, every one of them pretty.

Soon I went back to Uncle Tom. "Look a here, when I got home that hog had done been there and went up under the shelter and straight back to her bed."

"I started to tell you that but I decided to let tricks work."

That was years ago. After that sometimes I'd set around there half a day talkin with him. "Women come from fur and near and want me to tell them what made them sick was their best friend have tricked them. I won't do it," he say. "What have tricked them was wearin low-neck dresses and silk stockins through the wintertime. They got their body full of cold."

Leavin his house one evenin, why, I don't know, but it just

come to me: I could do what Uncle Tom do. I started usin voodoo—or makin like I was usin it—to give people encouragement.

I tried to help my sister-in-law Doll. She was young and sporty and courtin another lady's husband. After Doll and this old lady fell out, Doll say, "Ed, that woman come through my yard most every day. I don't want her comin through here."

"You scared of her?"

"Yeah, I wonder ain't she workin roots or puttin down somethin for me to step on. I think I'll put me a hole in a dime and string it around my leg, so if she tries to conjure me, the dime will turn black."

"I'll tell you what to do. Next time she come, run right out there with a shovel and take up her tracks and throw them over the house. Be sure she see you do it."

It worked. When the old lady seed this she never pass through there no more.

Such as this was against me when I try to get my wife to go to Dr. Acton. Seem like I the man believe in hoodoo and didn't believe in it. I thought if I eased around and let her sisters and her ma take my wife to root workers, they'd find out for theyselves Willie Mae had to go to the hospital.

Mrs. Sparrow want me to carry my wife to Uncle Tom.

"Come on in," he say. "I knowed you had trouble and I been lookin for you all day."

He was settin in a chair with a ball of roots wrapped in thread and hangin from a cord about seven inches long. I tell him I was wantin to find out what to do for my wife.

Every time he pose a question he'd tell the roots, "Cross me," and them roots would go crost him. Or, he might say, "If that be true, come to me." They'd come right on. If they move sort of slow, Uncle Tom would cuss and say, "Come on up here."

Mrs. Sparrow ask, "Who tricked Willie Mae?"

"Well, she tricked all right. Don't take no root worker to see that. But she ain't been tricked by a man. That for sure." My heart quieted down. "I can't help you," Uncle Tom say. We taken my wife on home.

We had a dog named Shep—half bull and half police—that really loved her. Lots and lots of times she'd talk to him for a couple of hours at a time, just like she was talkin to somebody. Sometimes she'd go lay down in the pasture and wouldn't get up. Shep would stay right with her.

Once I went off to Rochelle. The first thing I heard when I got back to Abbeville was she had burnt down a telegram pole.

It got so all the white people was at me about sendin her to the hospital. "When you gonna send off Willie Mae, Ed?"

One evenin Dr. Acton stop me on the street. "I seen Willie Mae going into the root worker's house the other day."

"Yes, sir."

"Ed, those crooks can't help her."

My wife's sisters and her ma carried her from one root worker to another. Back and forth. Spendin my money. Burnin my gas. Eatin my food. They was about to drive me crazy.

After I heard them talkin about carryin my wife to Mac Baldwin I taken him three dollars lackin a very little change. "Yeah," he told them, "Willie Mae tricked all right. She need to go to the state hospital and I'll work on her there."

A person who has lost they mind can really vex you. If I went to town in the car, she would walk. To keep her from walkin I'd start out ahead. She'd pass me on the road and not pick me up. Most evenins she would just cook for herself.

Once she put boards acrost the windows and the back door and nailed them up and then turned the only lock we had, the one on the front door. I tear a window open and climb in.

One time I clean forget myself. I come in from work. No supper. No hot water. No nothin. She had fixed her some supper and she was settin right there by the kitchen door eatin it. The minute I come in she commence to fussin. I forgot all about her mind. I haul off and slap her. She look surprised.

Time I done it, I knowed I done wrong. She run away from

there like someone after her. I couldn't catch her. She hop on the truck and went and got the sheriff.

He come out there with a warrant and arrest me.

"I'm ready to go," I say.

"No. Just pay your bail and stay home."

I had to go to court. The judge say, "Ed, they got you for slappin your wife."

"Yes, sir, I slapped her all right."

"Well, give me forty-five dollars and keep your hands to yourself."

She couldn't figure why they wouldn't lock me up. I had always said that when a lady try to put me in jail she was through eatin my food. But I kept my wife right on.

She got mad and move over to her ma's. I went over there one day and her ma and her sisters had her tied to the bed and both feets to the bottom. "Let her up. You all is goin to let her up this minute." And I untie her. I guess she had got to raisin sand and that was all they knowed to do with her.

Mrs. Sparrow say she aimin to carry my wife to a root worker named Ma Thomas at Unadillo that afternoon. I got in my truck and went straight to Ma Thomas. I bought right smart of her medicine and she promise to tell Mrs. Sparrow to send my wife to the hospital.

When I carry my wife and her ma there that afternoon Ma Thomas reach in my wife's clothes and felt her stomach, "Well, her stomach's full of conjuration. Why don't you send her to the hospital and I'll work on her there?"

She give my wife some clear medicine with a mustard leaf floatin around in it. "Here. Take this when you get to the hospital."

Then Mrs. Sparrow ask Ma Thomas could she hurt someone beatin on a log.

"Yes, Lord, if I wills it, I can get a person so sore he can't hardly move tomorrow." Ma Thomas draw a piece of wood out the fire. "Don't say nothin aloud, just name to yourself the one you want to hurt. Now put your finger on the log." Mrs. Sparrow touched it. "That place goin to be the head of the person you want to hurt. You ain't aimin to kill them, is you? I won't knock the head so as not to kill nobody. There's somebody mean goin to be so sore they can't hardly move tomorrow."

Ma Thomas went to beatin on the log. Mrs. Sparrow couldn't hardly look at me. I suspicion I the one she tryin to hurt.

I took Mrs. Sparrow and my wife home and goes to see Dr. Acton. It had been the better part of two years now since he told me to send my wife to the hospital. I tell him about the root workers and how I couldn't get nobody in the family to sign the papers for the hospital, about me slappin my wife, and her threatenin with a butcher knife. I ask him what should I do.

"Go home. I'll help you."

That afternoon the high sheriff—he was distant related to Dr. Acton—come to my mother-in-law's and call me and my daughter out. If he had just talked to me by myself, everyone in my wife's family would claim I was tellin a big story. I really was proud my daughter was there.

"Ed," the sheriff say, "go home. Don't put your foot over here to your mother-in-law's again. Don't send no groceries and no money. Don't put out nare 'nother penny on no root worker. Do, I'm goin to put you in jail."

How come he to do this? Could this be the Lord speakin? He don't come down here and talk no more. He could have put his word to someone else with authority.

I went on home and the very next day my wife's brother come. "We ready to send Willie Mae off."

Just then the high sheriff driv up in my yard. "I'm supposed to carry you all to the doctor's. He want to see you. And Willie Mae's sister and her brother too. Right now."

When all of us got there Dr. Acton look straight past us, straight out the window at the square. He start talkin soft. Willie Mae got to go to the hospital. The way he suggest is the only way. Now his voice rise up. The root workers not only ain't goin to do no good but they is pointedly against her case. When he talk about them Dr. Acton make a ball out of the paper on his desk and just as hard as he can he throwed it in the waste basket. Bam! We should all get together and go acrost to the courthouse this afternoon—don't wait for tomorrow—and sign the papers. Do we want the sheriff to go with us or can we go by ourselves?

The rest of them select to go by ourselves. We sign our names and now after a hearin before some doctors my wife can go to the hospital.

About two weeks later me and the sheriff take her there. When the sheriff come for us Shep try to get in the car with my wife. The sheriff told him, "Go on way from here." He cry so pitiful and look like he couldn't hardly stand to see my wife leave. Her ma was standin to the window. She had throwed her apron over her face.

Down the highway we went, my wife rhymin words, one right after another like she had been doin all day long sometimes.

When the sheriff driv up to the state hospital two great big women nurses come out to the car. They didn't say "Howdy" or nothin. One of them look at me and say, "This is a man. We don't handle men. We just suppose to be sent after womenfolks."

I knowed right then they thought I was the one sick. I was feelin down at the very bottom of the world and I reckon them nurses thought I was lookin worser than my wife.

"No, I ain't the one sick. It's my wife."

"Here she is," one of the women say. She went towards my wife. From young on up my wife had been a little lady and now she had fallen off to where she was real skinny. They bore down on her just like they was goin at a snake.

"Don't handle her so rough." I wanted them to treat her like she was people. "She ain't goin to hurt you."

They ease up a little and took her on in the hospital. She

didn't say good-by or nothin. Me neither. Just when she got to the door she turnt around like she was wantin to ask me where she goin.

The sheriff carried me home. Just outside Abbeville he stop and went to the shed behind the Owl Café and bought him some moonshine. When he come out he say, "Ed, if you want some whiskey, go get it." Well, he was the sheriff. I bought me a pint. It was pretty fair stuff. But it wouldn't take holt. Seem like the bottom of my stomach had fell out.

About every two weeks I'd carry some snuff and some watermelons in season and bananas and apples to my wife. Once just as I driv up to the hospital I had a blowout. So I took the lug bolts off one wheel. I wasn't payin no attention and they rolled down through the bars over the sewer.

"What am I goin to do now?" I ask myself out loud.

A man standin at the window behind bars say, "Well, I'll tell you. There are five or six lugs on every wheel. You just need four. Go around to each one and take off some lugs. Then you'll have some to take the place of the ones that got away from you."

I look at him. "You're supposed to be *crazy*. And you got more sense than I is."

Them people don't just set down. Willie Mae worked in the dinin room and kitchen settin tables and washin dishes.

Whenever one ain't got no family or his folks won't come get him and he can get well enough that he can go all over town, they put him out and trust him to work for other folks. Late in the evenin you'll see them carryin they pocketbooks comin back to the hospital just like it was really home.

You can ask about some of them and learn they come there by spells. There awhile and home awhile.

They gets scared there. They won't tell you nothin and talk right low. My wife had dark spots under her eyes. Her hair was packed down on her head. It hadn't been combed. She wasn't cleaned up like she should have been. It made me mad. I tell the nurse I want to see the doctor.

"You ain't got an appointment," she say. "You can see him the next trip."

In two weeks I was back there. "Doctor, seem like my wife's goin down. I love my wife. I didn't bring her here to throw her away or to get shut of her."

"If you think so much of her, why in the hell didn't you keep her at home?"

"Dr. Acton told me this was the onliest place that I could bring my wife to get help."

"Boy, I believe you do love your wife. So I'm goin to do the best I can for you."

They will put your people back if you don't go and talk up for them. They wasn't seein my wife at all until they seed I was carin for her. The next time I talk with the doctor seem like I got on his nerves.

"You got to help me."

"Anything I can," I say.

"Go home and keep your shirt on, and I'll send your wife home to you. You come back up here *every* two weeks and it take me two weeks to get her straightened out after you come. If you want to know anythin, write me; I'll write you."

The welfare office sent for me. They had a letter from the hospital. They commence to tell me about signin papers to get my wife shock treatments and I tell them I don't want to sign nothin to put my wife in the hospital no tighter than she is 'cause I want to get her out.

"Well, Ed, they got to have them papers signed so they can take care of her and they gonna get her well so she can come back." They kept on talkin to me ("You don't want her to come back out there and you wake up with your head cut off, do you?") and I sign the papers.

About two more weeks the doctor write me again. Miss Lacey read all my mail for me while my wife was in the hospital.

"This say you can come get Willie Mae. Now ain't that nice."

I went at my wife on the bus. She come out smilin. I say, "Us gonna get together and live and forget all that old past."

For about ten years after she come home from the hospital, me and my wife got along good.

Ma King was the first person I ever knowed to take dope. Dr. Acton the second. When he come to Abbeville he was a real nice-lookin young man, slim built and dressed nice. Before they got so many kids his wife'd ride around with the doctor, especially when he made calls at night.

If you went out to the car, she'd cover her face with her hands. If you went to Dr. Acton's house, she'd come and open the door but she'd stand behind the door and talk to you. The colored got to askin, "How come she won't let nobody see in her face?"

He kept his car full of kids all the time. They was a jumpin bunch and it look like he really enjoy them. Him and his wife had this colored girl for a nurse, and when the kids went with him, she went too. The girl got to comin out front with a baby.

I don't know whether the rumor was amongst the whites or not, but it was amongst the colored that it was Dr. Acton's baby. It got back to his wife. She took to followin him around by goin with him in the car. Then the girl would be home takin care of the kids.

One fellow told me, "I'll bet you my head that's Dr. Acton's baby."

I say, "I don't believe it. Dr. Acton is a doctor. He ain't goin to let that girl have no baby and scandalize his name like that."

When the girl got in labor Dr. Acton's wife gets in the car and goes with the doctor. When the baby was born Mrs. Acton was settin right there. He was a black chile, even blacker when he was first born than his mother was. Mrs. Acton taken a long look at that baby, got up, and went out and set in the car and waited for the doctor.

At his office Dr. Acton had a waitin room in the front for whites and a waitin room in the back for colored. He'd tell it to you straight whatever was wrong with you.

I went to him about a pain between my shoulders. From the time I was about ten I had to hold up cotton to be weighed in the field. Two people, one at each end, squat down and raise the cotton up off the ground. A man can let the stick rest on his shoulder. But a small boy won't be high enough. So I had to put it on my head.

One time when I did that a pain went right down my neck bone and my back. I thought my neck was broke. Ever since then I've had pains sometimes between my shoulders.

Dr. Acton say, "Ed, that's just somethin you got to live with."

There is some drugs that when a doctor give that stuff out he got to give the names of the ones he givin it to. He must have been overusin it 'cause him and his wife got hooked.

The way he got caught up with was the FBI took them names and the agents went around to see the people and they hadn't bought any drugs and didn't know nothin about it.

Everybody like Dr. Acton. You know how some people just likable. He was nice talkin, nice to everybody. All the colored was crazy about him. If he had ask them to help him out, not to say nothin, a heap of people would have been too glad. But he didn't do that. The government caught him and he had to go off to prison for twelve months.

Before he went he had plenty of money and a nice big farm with twenty-five or thirty head of cattle. While he was off, people strip his farm of cows and everythin else they could go off with.

When he come back the spirit was knocked out of him. He got so he wouldn't go to the office worth nothin. Two o'clock in the afternoon he wouldn't be there.

I went there one day and his office was as dirty and nasty a place as you ever seed.

"Doc, what's happened? Why don't you hire someone to clean it up?"

"I can't hire no one. I'm the brokest doctor you ever knowed."

He had got so he wouldn't bathe. And he had growed a beard. Some said he had a cancer. We was settin there talkin, "Why don't you shave?"

"Well, I'll tell you. I leave that on so the women won't bother me, but two or three of them hang on still.

Not long after that he went out to his farm bird huntin and they found him settin in his car dead. He couldn't have been over forty, hardly that old.

15 The men workin for Mr. Addison thought he made a bad mistake when he turnt under an old cemetery for chain gang people. The cemetery took up an acre of ground right in the middle of a big field. We had been plowin up to the cemetery with mules and goin around it. It was all over with plum trees.

"Clean it up," Colonel Addison told us. "I want to turn that cemetery into a field."

He had us to pull them trees up and to take his tractor and to plow the cemetery all in. Some of the boards was pulled off the caskets.

Them convicts had been whipped and knocked and killed. Cap'n Smith was the chain gang warden and he'd get drunk and go to beatin. The people on the chain gang thought an awful lot of Miss Smith. When she heard them callin on the Lord and cryin for mercy she'd make him stop.

He'd wait for her to go to town or off fishin and then he'd really cut someone up.

Finally they pass a law to take the strop off the chain gang. The wardens wasn't suppose to beat the convicts anymore. But Cap'n Smith did it right on. He would have a man lay across a barrel and have one man hold the head and another the feets of the man he was going to beat.

Then he'd go to it. It's pretty bad to hear a fellow fastened down beggin for mercy. That'll make anybody feel bad.

Then our preacher told us some higher ups had finally got after him about the beatin he was doin. So he found other ways to punish the convicts. Sometimes he would have them sit on somethin sharp. Then he would put they hands and they heads and they feets in a stock. And put syrup on they faces. The flies would come.

If you don't believe it worry a man to kill people, you should have heard Cap'n Smith when he died. Miss Smith sent for my wife to come help her.

"I ain't goin over there less'n you come," my wife say. So I went. We had to hold Cap'n Smith on the bed. He was scared of the things he was seein. When anybody would ask him what was the matter he'd say, "Them niggers is at me."

One of the hands, Lawse Johnson, wouldn't have nothin to do with workin the days we turned under the cemetery. He claim he was bad sick.

"I don't think Mr. Addison ought to bother them people," Lawse said. "With all the land he got he could let them rest and not stir the dead.

Just about a year after he plow up the convict cemetery Mr. Addison lost what little hair he had lef and all his teeth. Him and Mrs. Addison traveled from one doctor to another. After a while he decide to stay home.

Us hands dug the graves for Mr. Addison's mother and father in the Abbeville cemetery. Mr. Addison had they bodies dug up and brought where he was.

"It had got to where Mr. Addison was worried was his parents' graves being taken care of up north," Mrs. Addison said.

It was the custom if the landlord was dyin when the crop was sold to settle with his wife or his son after the funeral. But Mr. Addison didn't want that. He was propped up in the bed lookin even whiter than ever. "Let all the boys come here and settle. Forgive them their old debts and let them start new. I want them to be satisfied."

Mr. Addison died. Mrs. Addison call us hands together. "I'm goin to run the place right on and you all can settle down and anybody who wants to can stay with me."

I never seed Mrs. Addison in a rage the whole years I worked for them. You'd tell her your story. "Do you really need that?"

"Yes'm, Mrs. Addison, I sure do. Pretty bad."

"You ain't goin to play cards with it?"

I'd have to tell her I want it to get me somethin to eat. Or for overalls.

She'd always let me have it. I would be there talkin to Mrs. Addison and Miss Berk'd dash up. "I ain't goin to let you kill Rayburn,"—that was Mrs. Addison's name—"you all kilt Mr. Addison." (She was 'ferrin to us hands comin there at money.)

Before Mr. Addison died I got to doin my business with him. Now I want to talk with Mrs. Addison. It was always best to do your business with the boss. I never knowed a good overseer. And the Addisons and Miss Berk had some sure enough bad ones, Mr. Lindley in particular.

He worried me to death movin me from one house to another. He was a white man crazy about colored women—crazy about them—and he liked Carrie best. She was a brown-skinned, slim little lady, right pretty. But her long hair didn't look alive but dead. She kept it balled all around her head—grease was what she use on it.

For about ten years she was married to a good friend of mine named Butler Anderson. He quit the Baptists and got sanctified with the Holy Rollers. When Butler took up the collection he'd sing over and over:

> *"If all these people were Jesus's people*
> *What a glorious time it would be."*

He wanted me to get sanctified too, but I never did. It hurt me to my heart for him not to take up time with me 'cause I wasn't sanctified. Soon, he left Carrie and took a sanctified wife. Carrie and her three chillen move in with Charlie Samson. Saturday Charlie would go to the market in town. There in a box would be the butcher's scraps, the skin and bones and the very little meat that hangs on to them when the meat is cut to put in the counter. I never did like to buy it 'cause people spits in it. He'd take that stuff home and Carrie would cook it to eat.

Once Charlie steal a full sack of flour, a two-gallon bucket of lard, and five pounds of sugar out of my house, but I caught him 'cause he had a strain halted mule that made strange tracks by twistin his feet and diggin out the dirt. I knowed Charlie had visited me when I saw them tracks.

I follow them back to Charlie's house and told him somebody had stole my groceries.

"Why don't you go to Aunt Jane?" he say.

"Why I want to go to a root worker? I know exactly who got my groceries."

But I went to Mrs. Addison to get some money to go to Aunt Jane. Some claim if the sheriff wanted to know where somethin was, he'd ask her.

Mrs. Addison say, "Ed, Aunt Jane's a big old woman and she ain't going to do nothin but have you drink tea and then she'll have you to turn the cup upside down and she'll go to guessin. I don't think you ought to put no stock in what she say. Her word won't stand up in court. Course, if you want the money, I'll let you have it."

When I told Aunt Jane about my meat she say, "You gonna have a long life. You gonna be a well liver and own a real nice automobile and some land. The very best of your land is goin to be west of your house. Someone close around you broke in and took your meat."

I went to the overseer. "Mr. Lindley, Charlie stole my food."

"How do you know? That little guy's goin to be mighty mad when you tell him that."

"I was mighty mad when he got my groceries too."

"I'll find them."

I wait all week for Mr. Lindley to find those groceries. But he didn't do it. Saturday come and when Charlie and his family went to town I went to his house and pick up my food. We never had no conversation about it.

I was livin on one of the Addison farms and workin on another. My house with a good stand of trees in front was off by itself. If Carrie move there, then, Mr. Lindley figured, he'll be able to visit her while Charlie off workin with no one seein him come and go. "Ed, don't you want to move down there on that place where you're workin at?"

Later that evening I tell Mr. Lindley, "No, my wife say she don't want to go down there."

"You'll have to go there or go somewhere else 'cause I done let Charlie Samson have your place."

I knowed there wasn't nothin I could do about it. "Well, I'll take it if you let me carry my mule that I been workin down there with me."

"All right."

I got my wagon and put my things on it and throw my baby up on top and call my dogs up and tie my cow behind the wagon. All this time my wife was sayin she wasn't goin. When I start off and she seen I was really goin, she say, "Where my place up there?" I fix a place for her and she got on up and we moved.

Soon a new highway was built about twenty-five feet in front of the house we had left, the trees was cut down, and Mrs. Addison built a fillin station a little piece from the back door. It was too public a place now to suit Mr. Lindley.

So he figure on puttin Carrie in the place we had just moved to. He measure the house. It leak and he goin to cover it with shingles for Carrie.

She come over and put out a fret about what her and Charlie was goin to do there next year. They was goin to have them some pretty flowers. And they was goin to build a porch. This make my wife very mad. "I'm tired of Carrie comin over here and throwin out big hints about what she goin to do."

I was dissatisfied. I hated to do it but I figured on leavin.

After Mr. Addison died Mr. Benny Abraham was the head man seein at Mrs. Addison's business. One Saturday evenin I pass Mr. Addison's office. Mr. Abraham call me. There was an iron vault in the office that you could walk in that was a straight room. To tell you the truth, I was sorta scared. I hadn't never been in there before. Mr. Abraham say, "I hear you goin to move."

"I am goin to move due to the conditions I have been working under."

"What are they?"

"I ain't on the chain gang but Mr. Huey Lindley totes a 32 Smith and Wesson pistol in his pocket and he has got a ax handle he bored a hole in and made just like a policeman's club."

"You won't have to work under him next year. We're goin to get shut of him but we don't want him to know it before he get through gatherin. What I tell you is only for you to know. Do you understand?"

"Yes, sir."

I left out of there a happy man. Now when Mr. Lindley come to my house, "Help yourself," I tell him, "measure anything you want."

Two months after the crops was gathered Mr. Lindley get the message he have to move. I goes over to Kramer Sunday mornin to be with the rest of the boys. As I get in sight I seed Mr. Lindley's car settin in the road and about fifteen hands standin around it. Mr. Lindley say, "Here come old Ed. You better come on up and get this last drink with me. It's the last one you'll have less'n you're goin to move with me." He give me his bottle and I took me a good drink of shine. We stand there about half an hour talkin.

That evenin Mr. Lindley come to my house and tell me he has traded for a big farm with a man at Ryan. He want me to move with him. I say, "I have done told Mr. Benny Abraham I'm goin to stay on here with Mrs. Addison."

"Is you goin to stay here with that Christ-killin son of a bitch?" (Mr. Abraham is a Jew and that is what Mr. Lindley was 'ferrin to.)

"Yes, sir."

He turnt red and whirl around and lef me.

Workin for Mrs. Addison, I was on shares. When the crop was laid by I would work some for wages, but I could quit anytime I took a mind to. In my garden I had ripe watermelons, roastin ears, peas, butter beans, and all kinds of vegetables.

Then, at that time of year, a lot of people wouldn't have jobs.

And along about August most of them ain't got no garden much, except maybe some turnips they sowed in a shady place and maybe some white potatoes or sweet potatoes.

Our friends from town and my wife's family would come and eat everythin we had except hay. It was always best to take them fishin so they could eat what they caught.

We used to go in a crowd to the river bank and cook all we caught and eat it. My mother-in-law, Mrs. Sparrow, was lucky enough to catch two bluegill perch, about one and one-half pounds apiece, that the government had put in the river. We got ready to cook. I don't think she wanted to share.

No, she not goin to eat, she got gas on her stomach, and she don't want no dinner, she goin to take her fish back home. We eat with a lot of jolly jolly about ain't this good, just to make her hungry. Next time I seed her she say she wished she had cooked her fish and eat it at the river 'cause when she got home it was tainted.

Long about July or August when the creek was dryin up and the fish would go to the deepest hole, white and colored would get together and muddy the water. Then the fish would stick they heads up and you could catch them with your hands.

The Ocmulgee River and its swamp was the main place for huntin and fishin in Wilcox County, Georgia. It belong to the government, but many of the people that own land wouldn't let you go through their property to get to it.

Jordon's Bluff was a good place but the colored couldn't fish there. Neither at Poor Robin, the big spring where the white people had camp houses and went in swimmin. There wasn't no swimmin place for the colored in Wilcox County.

The water at Poor Robin was as clear as glass and you could see eels and big fish. Us colored was allowed to fish around it though mostly not in it. Some of the whites ownin property would ask you to leave. If they didn't say nothin to you, they'd write a note that the colored wasn't allowed to fish there and put it in your car.

One day I was fishin near Poor Robin when Mr. Jake

Monroe come by. "Ed, what bait you usin?" He allows worms is all right but grasshoppers is better.

"Yeah? How you catch them?"

"Get you a five-bushel oatsack. Sew the top around a hoop to keep it open. Fasten it on your truck low onto the ground. Drive over the pasture and when the grasshoppers fly up out of the way of the truck the sack will catch them."

I usually caught grasshoppers by knockin them out with a fly swatter and puttin them in a fruit jar with holes in the lid.

When the river got high and overflowed, the carp would come where you could see, and then me and Mr. Jake could gig them with three-pronged pitchforks.

Mr. Jake knowed the swamp from Abbeville to Cedar Creek. He could go through it on the darkest night as good as I could in the daytime. It seem like as long as he stay in it the swamp lift some of Mr. Jake's troubles from him.

He could hit a pin on a post or turn a match or cut a thread with a bullet. He hardly ever missed a bird if he was in a fair place. And he knowed where many a covey of quails lived. A quail is just like a chicken. It has got a roostin place and a feed range where it stays. Every year Mr. Jake would go to them places and find him some birds.

Goin to the swamp in different seasons is like lookin at the same woman at different times. She can sure surprise you by how unlike she look than when you seed her before. Me and Mr. Jake went to the swamp in all seasons.

It's huntin season in January and February. The birds are there but you won't see many squirrels. In March and April people are plantin they crops and gardens. They're not in the swamp much to watch the leaves buddin out green and the plum and dogwood and crabapple trees bloomin.

By May everythin has come out in full force. Now the people come. Some of them don't stay still. The animals won't come if they get the scent of you.

Day or night there is no stirment of air. If you want fruit, the plums in the orchards on the edge of the swamp are hard, not so good to eat but they make good jelly. The blackberries end in May or June just before the blueberries and gooseberries come. You find them on the hill side of the swamp. Now in July the honeysuckle vine smells sweet and every bird want to sing. So Mr. Jake learnt me the swamp. And I learnt him. A lot of people call him mean but me and Mr. Jake could make it good. The first time I seed him he was a red-headed baby. He wouldn't go to school much. He growed to be a turrible strong man, and if anyone treat him wrong, they had trouble on they hands. He made the best policeman we ever had in Abbeville. He would protect the colored just like the white, so they soon got shut of him. Just when it come up about him lockin up the whites as quick as he would the colored, he killed a white fellow who come there drinkin.

Mr. Jake killed in self-defense. If the man had been colored, nothin would have been said. But the dead man's relatives got him fired.

One time drinkin stump on the way to get a pint apiece at Hawkinsville, Mr. Ridley tell Mr. Jake what this person and that person had said about him.

When he come back home Mr. Jake start out with a pistol in one hand and his pint in the other. He walked from fillin station to fillin station. Everyone in town was giving him plenty of room. He didn't have no troubles with the law or any of the rest of them 'cause they knew he was drunk and that he was goin to shoot that pistol. He had to pay a big fine for cuttin up in town.

He had further trouble. Some of the white people was sellin tickets for one dollar apiece for a chance on a bale of cotton they was goin to give away at a Halloween party to help the white school library. Some of the colored bought tickets. "You don't have to be there to win."

They brought the cotton to where they was goin to give it away. Unloadin it, Mr. Jake and Mr. Sanford had some words and Mr. Jake beat Mr. Sanford so bad he had to go to the hospital. He never was the same again. It affected his brain. Mr.

Sanford was sort of a big man 'cause his daddy-in-law was a big man.

Mr. Jake was bad worried. I think Mr. Jake had pretty good confidence in me. I give him the best ideas I had. We was settin where the creek run into the lake behind Piney Grove Church fishin. And we saw a mink get in the water on the other side of the lake with a full-grown rabbit in his mouth. We set there watchin the mink and then he say, "Ed, I'm thinkin about goin overseas 'cause I can get a job earnin two hundred a month or more."

"I don't want you to go. You're worth more than that to us here. You're the one who's holdin the whole thing together." And the truth was I did want him to stay. Him bein my friend kept the other whites off me. They was scared of him.

I told him, "If you keep a goin to town and fightin and payin out fines, the day will come when they'll get you in a fight to make you pay. Nobody help you fight and nobody help you pay, do they?"

"That's right."

I tried to help him 'cause he had helped me. He was, I believe, as good a white friend as I had there as I know of. If he was drunk I could say, "Come on, Mr. Jake," and he would come right on and I would take him home.

The last time I seen him, me and him went wild hog huntin. I never was lucky enough to tie up with a wild hog, but Mr. Jake would find one sometimes and he'd give it to me. On the farm we would trim the tushes off hogs to keep them from damagin other animals. Not Mr. Jake. He would lay a hog down and shoot them off with a 38 pistol. "That the best way to do it," he say. Seem like shootin anythin made him feel easier.

Before Mr. Addison died he got down too sick to see at his farms, so he tried to sell. A big rich Yankee called Mr. Hatfield come to see did he want to buy. He took a mind to go bird huntin. I was one of the colored Mr. Addison had to go with him.

Miss Belle Vaughn, the white lady who delivered mail in

Abbeville, not regular but like a substitute, come along. Before they was old enough to be turnt loose with a gun, she used to take her nephews around to target practice on robins. They will cluster over a chinaberry tree so thick you can get five or six with a shotgun.

Miss Vaughn used to fish a lot with Miss Sadie Smith, the wife of Cap'n Smith, the chain gang warden. Miss Smith checked on your light meter. She didn't hunt regular, so I think she come along that day to look at the millionaire.

Mr. Hatfield had a 22 rifle and I was wonderin what was he goin to do with it. A rifle not shootin but one bullet at a time, you got to hold it dead on the target. For a 22 rifle you could get about fifty shots for seventy-five cents, but it take a mighty good marksman to kill a rabbit or anythin that move with a rifle, particularly birds and wild fowl. To get a wild turkey you near about have to stay in the woods long enough to smell like one.

Most anybody can hit good with a shotgun 'cause the shots scatter. For some birds you can use a shotgun with light number eight shots. But for a shotgun you don't get but twenty-five shots for three dollars.

"What birds do you hunt here?" Mr. Hatfield ask me.

"I have eat everythin but mockinbirds. They just set around and sing and don't nobody bother them. And bluebirds."

I learnt him what I could about our birds, how the sapsucker eat ants, and about the redhead leavin us in the winter, and when you see it you know you can go ahead and plant even though mornins are still cool. The yellowhammer pick a hole in a dead tree and lay a nest there. In March and April the black-birds come in droves to fill up on corn. They fly from field to field and we shoot them in droves with a shotgun. You can put them in a pie. Doves and sparrows make fine pies too. "Maybe they're not for someone livin high," I tell him, "but for a poor man they're mighty good eatin."

"We have quail aplenty. And a hunter can hide in the peanut field and kill doves as they come in or hide by a water hole in fall when things dry up."

"You seem to know all about huntin here."

"I have to keep my family eatin."

Mr. Hatfield got a whole bag of birds that day. He hardly miss any he shot at.

I heard Miss Vaughn tell Miss Smith, "Well, he may be a millionaire but he get as much meat for his shells as any poor man I ever seed."

Mr. Hatfield ask me had I ever seen inside a possum's pouch. I tell him the openin is about the size of a silver dollar. The bottom is much larger, like a sack gathered up at the top. There's fur and tits in there.

"Not enough tits," he say.

A possum is different from other milk-givin animals. The tit swells up in the little one's mouth and you can't unconnect the baby no how until it's through drinkin milk for good. It hang on there for about three months.

The she possum has got more babies than she got tits. Every one quick enough to beat the others to a tit keeps it. The rest of them starve to death.

"Well, I've never counted the tits," I tell him. But I have caught she possums that had four or five young ones about a quarter grown swingin to her back—that's what they do when they gets big enough to leave off drinkin milk—and a set of little ones about an inch long in her pouch.

He say he had studied animals right smart and that he didn't think that was right.

"Well, it sure is."

"You'll hear from me on that." He ask my name.

"Ed."

"Ed what?"

"Ed Brown."

"Well, Mr. Brown, when I get home I'll find out about that and let you know."

It was the first time a white person ever called me Mister. Every time I thought about it after that I smiled to myself. I liked it.

Miss Vaughn and Miss Smith looked at each other and at the ground. They was too humble to Mr. Hatfield to laugh.

About two weeks after he went back north the postmistress sent for me. "Ed, you know who Mr. Brown is?" she ask me.

I didn't say nothin.

"Here's a letter for you. Sent care of the postmaster. Look like folks don't know who's runnin things around here."

"No'm."

"Well, speak up, boy. You want me to read it to you?"

"Yes'm."

The letter told how I was right about the possum. Mr. Hatfield wrote he had looked in a book and it told how in the south a possum can have two litters a year. But where it's cold she only has one.

"Lord, it look like some folks is just plain dumb." I thought she meant about a possum havin two litters. Then she say, "Callin a nigger mister!"

16 If there's a way to do it, people will come for Homecomin. You can meet many friends you couldn't meet no otherwise and the preacher will have them to get up and tell where they're livin and what they're doin.

At Homecomin we'd always leave three or four benches up front for the whites. When there was nothin but standin room in the church, whites would be standin on the pulpit.

"The colored got all the signs," Ardis say. Him and me was settin together. "It's bad luck to do this, bad luck to do that. And the whites got all the money. The white folks go to church for two hours and then go back home. If they want real good preachin and prayin and singin they got to come to the colored."

One year when the Piney Grove Church was crowded I seed the deacons standin in a ring. I walked up there and got in with them. The preacher was standin in the middle. I didn't know he was 'dressin these people. I thought they was tellin jokes. He tell them, "When you take up the collection, throw down two or three dollars and entice. That will make more folks strain theyselves. Afterwards you all that don't want to give can get your money back."

If you got a good friend and he call hisself a Christian in every way and you think he's a Christian and got confidence in him, don't watch him. I have known many a deacon and a chairman deacon and a preacher. I've watched them from young on up. My stepdaddy rented land. He could send me after a preacher with a mule and wagon because it was his own mule. So he had me haulin preachers this place and that.

The best man to trust is the Lord and not them. I believe in gettin on my knees. When I started a crop I wouldn't plow a furrow until I ask God to help me. I'd drag my plow down to the field and get on my knees and ask God to go with me.

You ain't got to go to church and make no big bull about it. But you got to have religion in your heart. If you vanish away from God, he'll vanish away from you.

In my church they thought I was too straight a man. The preacher say, "I want to make somethin out of Brother Brown. I believe he'd make a good deacon."

"No, don't ever make a deacon out of a stingy man," one of the deacons say.

I was always scared to fool the church in any way crooked. The church is always wantin somethin, a table, a rug, or somethin to be done. They knowed if they got me for deacon and they bought anythin, they was goin to have to tell the right price.

Dick Daniel bought a heater for the church. Every meetin he was askin about money for that heater. People got awfully tired of payin for it. They told him to carry it home.

The Evergreen Church hired an educated fellow named Reverend Foster for they regular pastor. The first Homecomin day after that, the members and they visitors was testifyin to tell what experiences they had had in Christian life. If somebody got up, like they had been before Reverend Foster come, and said, "The hell hounds runned me," he cut that off. But if someone talk about "I'm livin for the Lord and I'm gettin along good," he'd let that go on.

He would just stand there and talk like a teacher but he didn't have no voice to preach.

For Homecomin day the deacons ask Preacher Barker to come from Macon. He begin by sayin God didn't punish Job with sickness and sores 'cause he was mean. God was tryin to prove that He had more power than the Devil. The Devil put his hands on Job but couldn't touch his life because Job had faith. If you have as much faith as a mustard seed, in the long run you will overcome through God's power and righteousness.

Hold on to your faith. God's power is stronger than the Devil's. That's how Job overcome. Man, Preacher Barker sho' did preach. Everybody young and old was shoutin. The spirit had got 'em. He could sing and he could pray and he could mourn. He preached mournin. A lot of people in Preacher Barker's congregation come with him and worked with him to flush the sinners out of the pews and up to the front.

"Will you please come to Christ? Won't you come and be saved? Why not tonight?"

Reverend Foster didn't like that. The people didn't shout for him that a way. He couldn't touch Preacher Barker no way so he was jealous hearted and I think he was scared the visitin preacher would take his church—his livin—away.

When Preacher Barker start out the door I told him, "Man, you sho' went."

"I could have done better but my arm was painin me."

I looked and he had a broke arm there. And where the doctor had did it up it was sort of comin loose. I took and wrapped it back up for him. He went on back to the preacher's study and set there with the door open singin, hummin this, shoutin that, and every once in a while he'd drop down and swing and mourn, and Who—oo, it had the church in a rock.

Reverend Foster didn't come out like a preacher's due to do and say Preacher Barker done preached a wonderful sermon. He just went to preachin some hisself. He try to talk while the mournin was goin on. He couldn't drown it out. He got mad and quit.

Which one was right, the one that was givin all he had or the one that was just standin there not wettin his collar?

Sometimes a white fellow would come to our church to tell the farmers to join the Farm Bureau. "It used to be that the landowner could mortgage the whole crop. But the government has got it fixed now so you have to sign papers before the landlord can borrow on your half. And if you want to, you can borrow on your half separate from the boss's borrowin on his.

"Member how it was before the government went to sendin two separate checks, one to you and one to the boss? He could say, 'A check come. I cashed it and put your part on your debt.' "

The church was in a nod—"Yes, Lord."

Rogers Hollis was a deacon. He wouldn't help his wife get they chillen ready to go to church or help her carry them there. She got tired of this. The next time she got ready to go to church she dress the two chillen big enough to walk. Then she dress the baby and slip him into a clean guano sack and throw it across her shoulder. She didn't stop till she got to the Amen Corner.

When she put down her sack and taken the baby out of it the preacher stop preachin. Everybody look at her loaded down with them three little ones.

The preacher say, "Brother Hollis, is that your wife?"

"Yes."

"The next time she want to come to church, Brother Hollis, please help her."

One of the biggest things in a church was funerals. My wife was well knowed for helpin with them. She would bathe the body and help the family burn the bedclothes if a person died with a tedious disease.

The first funeral me and my wife ever went to together was Pete Nichols's. Just after we married he died. The last time I seen him he claim to be one hundred and four years old. In slavery time he was on a big plantation, he say, and they use him for gettin chillen, just like people have 'em a bull and breed cows. I always thought he was lyin, but he told it for the truth that that was his biggest job, just like it was a day's work.

Not everybody is sorry to see they people go.

At Crockerdale, Georgia, there was a woman with a heap of chillen. Her husband died of cancer. When the gravediggers start coverin the casket up, the woman grab a shovel from one of them and start throwin dirt: "I want to cover the rascal up."

How come she to act that way I don't know. Her husband was a hard worker. And it seem like he let her do about what she wanted. She had about as many chillen that didn't belong to him as did.

There was another lady—Mrs. Walker—me and my wife had tried to help some. She was sick, real sick, down in the bed. "I'm just waitin on the Lord." She had been settin at home six years, not doing nothin.

"Mr. Ed, I got a pain."

"Why don't you get up? Walk to the railroad today, to the trestle tomorrow. Soon you be goin to town."

Her husband used to run around a lot. I think the reason she stayed home was so she wouldn't see all that.

He got sicker than she was and died. She got up, cleaned up the place for him to be buried in the cemetery, and went all over town. It looked like him dyin filled her with new life.

The dead person's family not suppose to do nothin about washin the body or diggin the grave. The other relatives and neighbors will do that. Your family won't be allowed to bury you for twenty-four hours after you die. That's all right for people rich enough to use an undertaker, but any dead person who ain't embalmed soon start to stink, especially in the summertime.

Now they won't let you take a body in church unless it's embalmed. But back then they didn't embalm too much. Not the colored.

When he hear somebody's due to die the undertaker will be tiptoein around tellin the family, "Now let me know if anythin happen. I want to be all the help I can to you."

People will go to a funeral to see how is a fellow goin to put his folks away. After the service one will say to another, "They sure put Mr. So and So away nice."

The county will give you a burial in a flat box. If the family can't buy a tombstone, cups and saucers and shells will be used to mark the grave and to beautify it.

Sometimes in our settlement the church would be slam full for a funeral. A coin would be given to the usher to help the widow and chillen.

17 About two weeks before he died, me and Mr. Jack Wolfe was talkin. "You got a nice house. Why don't you paint it?"

"I ain't studyin about these earthly things. I'm tryin to make peace with God. I got a turrible hurtin in my breast."

I wasn't thinkin about him dyin but he did. The day before the funeral his oldest boy come and ask for help in diggin his daddy's grave. Then he mention his daddy had wanted a song sung over him. That throwed the fat in the fire; it was a stunnin thing. I knowed I couldn't lead it. I didn't know who amongst the colored was goin to be there. And the family was lookin for it to be sung.

When I got to the graveyard there was a white man I knowed bossin the diggin. I say, "Ain't it bad about Mr. Jack dyin?"

"No. I was goin to kill him if he didn't die soon or leave my daughter alone one." He had a daughter up about courtin size, about fourteen.

It hadn't been long happened that Mr. Jack had been sure enough beat up. He had been knockin around with a lady that come from a poor class of white people. When she got tired of him she jumped on him. One day Mr. Jack's mare come to my house with a bridle on and I took her home. Mr. Jack claim he got skinned up a little by bein thrown. It wasn't the mare that throwed him, I learnt.

All my friends amongst the gravediggers was laughin at me. I told them, "I ain't gonna sing no song. I'm goin down in the woods."

Ardis Griffen was there. Ardis never did live nowhere else but Mr. Jack's place till he went to the army. "What they want you to sing?" Ardis ask.

" 'Swing Low, Sweet Chariot.' "

"Yeah? Where the chariot gonna carry him?"

We was diggin and everybody was throwin in they thoughts. Some men be workin in the dirt all the time. If they wasn't able to change from work clothes to a suit, they wouldn't hardly go to church.

I see the wife and two little girls of Henry Sperry goin to church one night. "Where your daddy?" I ask the littlest girl.

"He can't go to church. He a naked nigger."

Maybe Mr. Jack'd let you have shoes or get you up somethin to wear if you didn't have sufficient clothes to attend church. In July when we had a revival Mr. Lark'd let us have money to pay the visitin pastor. And he was good about lettin you have his mules or his tools.

But he was bad about subsidy checks. I knowed all about how come J. W. Cromer to leave Mr. Jack after finishin one crop. Me and Mrs. Addison went to the AAA office when they handed out the government subsidy. When we got our check it was eighty dollars. Mrs. Addison give me forty.

Time I got back to my place, here come J. W. Cromer ridin a mule. He tended a two-horse farm for Mr. Jack and had got seventeen dollars subsidy.

"J. W., I got forty dollars."

He was lifted up when he come but when I show him my check for my one-horse crop and he didn't get but seventeen for his two-horse crop he knowed there was somethin wrong. He got right back on his mule and goes to Mr. Jack's house and tell him it look like he ought to got more out of his crop than that because Ed got forty dollars.

Mr. Jack say, "It's a damn lie. Ed didn't get that much."

"Yeah? I seed the check."

"Well, that's all you get out of yours." And it was.

I had just finished thinkin of J. W. when here come Mr. Jack's cousin, Mr. Raymond Wolfe, to see how was we gettin along with the diggin. Once Mr. Jack want me to help him nail on Jim Henry McEnglish what a heap of people laid to Mr. Raymond.

My wife had been missin things. We had covered half a hog
I got from the cold storage with red pepper and borax and meal
to keep bugs from it. I stored it in a box on a shelf in the
bedroom.

"There ain't no meat in that box," my wife told me.

"What?"

Someone had toted it all off except one piece. Soon Mr. Jack
come by and told me, "Ed, I found out who stole your meat."

"Did?"

"Jim Henry McEnglish. If you don't believe me, you can go
down there and ask Red's girls about it."

I knew Jim Henry had been knockin around with three
sisters. He didn't have no money to give them so he give them
my meat. I ask them what did the meat have on it.

"Red pepper and meal."

"Was it good?"

One say, "It sure was. But we didn't know it was your
meat." But they did because I seed them all the time and they
didn't tell me till after Jim Henry left from there. I soon found
out why Mr. Jack told me.

A lot of his property was open country. Between the railroad
and the highway he sowed five acres of oats. Two pretty heifers
of Mr. Raymond's got in it. When Mr. Jack tied tin cans to they
tails they had a fit and run away home. That was about an hour
to sun. Around nine o'clock that night Mr. Jack's barn burnt
down.

A bunch of colored fellows told me they seed Mr. Raymond
there early that evenin.

About a month later Mr. Jack say, "Ed, let's have Jim Henry
McEnglish arrested and get him back here. You tell the law he
stole your meat and carried it to Red's girls and I'll say he burnt
my barn down. That way the law will bring him back and put
him in the chain gang.

"Mr. Jack, that won't bring my meat back. If Jim Henry's
a thief, I don't want him around me. He'll get about twelve
months on the chain gang and he'll be right back out here stealin
again. Since he went off owin you, and since he stole my meat,

he won't hardly come back. We're shut of him like it is."

I sure suspicioned Jim Henry stole my meat. But I didn't know if he burnt Mr. Jack's barn. If I was to carry a man to court, I wanted it to be for somethin he did.

The day after we dug the grave was the funeral. I have noticed many times that if a white person die, they'll bury him pretty quick. They claim he'll turn black. If a colored person die, he already black. His family can keep him out a month and ship him all acrost the United States if they have a mind to.

I was feelin mighty small about singin that song. It sure give me a good feelin to see Honest Johnson come. And here come old Norman Dixon and his wife. They could sing. And Sun Fuller.

'I come to see is he really dead," Sun said.

He knowed Mr. Jack good. When the law come down on Sun and caught him with a barrel of buck that you make whiskey out of, they pour it out and lock him up. The fine is one hundred dollars and Mr. Jack pay it and get Sun out and tell him that he is under three years' probation.

For two crops Mr. Jack took everythin Sun made. Somebody told Sun he could move by findin him a bossman that would take up the probation in Mr. Jack's place. So Sun goes to Mr. Walter Ryan and Mr. Ryan say, "I'll go see after that." So, he goes to the courthouse and finds out Sun hadn't never been under no probation. Sun was a good hand and I reckon Mr. Jack figured if Sun thought he was under probation, he'd be scared to try to get on with anybody else.

Sun and me was the first of the colored—there was about twenty of us—in the church when the preacher ask did we want to view the body. There are two doors at the back of the church, one each side of the pulpit. We march in one door and up to the casket. Mr. Jack was real dressed up and look like he hadn't been sick a day.

"He dead all right," Sun say.

Sun come to work for Mr. Jack account of J. W. Cromer. Mr. Jack give J.W. money to tote around but he could not spend it. When J.W. got to town he show his money. "No, I can't lend you none of this," he tell Sun. "You go see Mr. Jack."

Sun went. When a hand is needed you can borrow money. Mr. Jack was a lot better to men he want to work on his place than he was to hands already on it.

One reason Mr. Jack had a hard time keepin hands after they move on his place was he had the fault of chasin colored women. Some men will not stand they women knockin around at all. Once they get in the winds of it they're gone. Some will take it for a while. But there's an old sayin that if you're foolin with a colored woman who's foolin with a white man you're drivin nails in your coffin.

Only a few white men that I knowed didn't go with a colored lady. From slavery till not so long ago it was hardly ever that you would meet a colored man able to more than support hisself. A man in the barber shop told it straight: "A colored lady will laugh and talk with a white man just as long as he want."

"Yeah, and when the colored lady makes a movie star or she get rich, she'll marry a white man," the barber say.

The general run of white men never owned up to they colored chillen. The white lady would know but she'd be scared to accuse her husband. She never would say nothin about it to him, I don't think.

All the neighborhood, white and colored, thought that Rosie Griffen, the colored lady that work for Mr. Jack, was goin with him. Her and him would go fix pasture fence together.

Them was panic times. Rosie was a widow with three chillen. She kept tellin me and my wife to come on over to her house. We hated to go 'cause we was afraid she didn't have enough food to feed us. When we got to her house she had a middlin and two hams hangin up. She really had more food than we had.

Goin home I reckon Rosie was more of a hustler than we knowed. My wife said, "Rosie well provided for, but it ain't the Lord takin care of her."

But when Miss Martha Tucker ask my wife about Rosie

Griffen and Mr. Jack courtin one another, my wife told her, "I don't believe it true. Folks just talkin."

It was best to tell a white person you didn't know nothin about such things. You can't hide what's come to the front but you can make like you don't see it.

After we view Mr. Jack layin in his coffin, lookin as good or, I'll even say, better than usual, us colored didn't set in the church to hear the funeral. We march toward the other door to the one we come in.

I don't think Mr. Jack went to the white folks' church much. But sometimes he'd go to Kramer Church, the colored church, and set in the meetin and pay a little, fifty cents or a dollar. And he went to the colored school closin. He love to be there, he say, and see how we would carry out the program.

As I was walkin out the church I seed Mr. Jack's boys and one girl, settin there fannin theyselves. Mr. Jack had tried to school them all but I don't know if nare one of them finished high school.

From the church door I pass through flowers standin up like a fence on either side of the green mat they had laid on the ground clean down to the grave, the most flowers ever I seed at a funeral.

When we come to the grave I was very glad to see Ruth Griffen, Rosie's daughter, standin there 'cause she like to sing. Rosie and her first two chillen, Ardis and his brother, is dark skinned. Ruth is about half as dark as they is. She was born on Mr. Jack's place.

I told her how the family was expectin Mr. Jack to be sung over and I didn't see how I was goin to do it. Ruth said she'd lead us in song if she could announce herself. "Just please yourself," I tell her, "as long as you sing."

When the time come she spoke out, "I been raised on Mr. Jack's place and I think I ought to have a right to sing a song over him."

The preacher and some of the other white folks spoke, "You're welcome to sing a song over him."

Ruth raise the song and all of us colored join in. We was bunched together and Ruth's brother, Ardis, and Chester Lemon and me was at the back.

Ruth begin, "Swing low, sweet chariot."

The rest of us join, "Comin for to carry me home."

Ardis bust out laughin so till he had to stoop down behind the rest of us and hide.

18 Wilmer was Mr. and Mrs. Addison and Miss Berk's butler for thirty years. One night after dinner, he told me, Mrs. Addison got to sneezin and went upstairs and didn't come down untill they brought her out in a casket.

That left me workin for her sister, Miss Berk. There was three of us on shares with her, me, my brother Homer, and Rogers Hollis.

Rogers was a liar. He was sort of an educated fellow and he could tell a heap sharper story than any of the rest of us. He goes to Miss Berk and tell her he want thirty dollars to buy a heap of cured meat cheap. She let him have the money.

Rogers's wife, Minnie Lee, work at Miss Berk's. Quite natural, Miss Berk ask, "How was that meat Rogers bought, Minnie Lee?"

"What meat? If he bought any meat he ain't brought none home."

The first of the month us tenants went to get furnish money. Miss Berk say, "Rogers, what did you do with the meat I give you the money to buy? Minnie Lee say you didn't bring it home."

He look cut down so bad. He lean up against the wall and took a deep breath. "Minnie Lee is such a wasteful woman. I was afraid to carry it home."

The rest of us knowed Minnie Lee hadn't never seen no meat to waste.

When I was leavin I say to Wilmer, "You reckon Miss Berk don't know Rogers?"

"Shoot!" he say, "she know him. If he had been by hisself she would have said more."

We knowed her, too. She would fuss just as big if you wanted a quarter as she would about lendin you one hundred dollars. She never sent me away without money if I asked for it. But not until she cried about not havin any. "What do you think I'm made of? Dollar bills?"

I'd just stand there and smile. Finally, she'd say, "Well, come on in here if you just got to have it."

The mornin Miss Berk ask Rogers about the meat, he stop in the yard and pick up a stick. Then he draw a circle on the ground. In the middle of that circle he sot up two low straws and one high straw. He bend the high straw over them two little straws. He was puttin hisself over Homer and me. I seed him do it.

Soon he got me in a fix where I had to tell a story myself. One day in town Rogers and me set on the curb with Mr. Powell, a real old colored man. He own three acres of land but he was too feeble to plow hisself. He made a deal to give us five dollars apiece to plant his peanuts.

He caught me by the arms. "Ed, you got plenty of strength. And you're young. Don't look at me and say how come *you* ain't got nothin? I let the chance go by. A chance is like a lady with a head full of hair comin toward you. You can catch her by the hair and hold her. Let a chance pass by and it like a bald-headed man—gone. You work hard. I want you to have somethin."

Saturday at sunup, keepin my word, I goes to Mr. Powell's and start workin. Rogers didn't come. About nine o'clock here come Wilmer from Miss Berk's house. Rogers had been there and told her I'm makin big money plowin some very hard land and that I'm fixin to strain her mules.

I wasn't supposed to be workin for nobody but her. When Wilmer takin me back to her house in the car, I ask, "What will I tell her?"

"I don't know. But you'll have to harden up and tell her somethin 'cause she is good and mad."

I want to stay on with her, so I take a little time to study. The last few weeks she had been so fussy she didn't seem to be her natural self.

This time when I got there I was standin around in the back waitin to see her, walkin along knockin my heels together. All of a sudden I run up on those straws Rogers had stuck in the ground.

One mind say, *There your trouble, right there.* I got on them things, stompin and kickin them into the ground.

From that minute things got better. When Wilmer call me to come see Miss Berk, I walk straight into the library.

"Miss Berk, Rogers and me both made this trade with old man Powell. Mr. Addison give us privileges by lettin us make money with the mules. In place of Rogers helpin me like he said, he come down here and tell you."

Now Mr. Addison had agreed if we was up with our crop we could take the mules and make us an extra dollar or two. But he hadn't told us we could go plowin no five acres of land. Miss Berk soften right up and give me the privileges I claim from Mr. Addison.

I went back to Mr. Powell's and finish the job. He paid me the whole amount of money he promised Rogers and me. I seed Rogers in town. "Seems like in place of tryin to help other people you try to trap them. How come you so dirty hearted?"

"I don't know why I to do that," he say.

I took my wife to a root worker and there was Rogers gettin his palm read. "Brown, you don't never have you hand looked over? I have mine looked over every year."

The first thing the new overseer, Mr. Jimmy Oates, did was to take away my mule. Miss Berk bought him a pair. One was awful fast and the other was awful slow. He give me the slow one and took my mule and he was a good 'un. I could plow with him from Monday sun to Saturday dinner just as hard as I could go.

"Don't worry," Miss Berk say, "if this mule Mr. Oates give you don't do you, I'll get you another."

She soon had to do that 'cause a stove fixer runned into him out on the road and broke his hind leg and we had to shoot him. Miss Berk told the Liberty stable to give me another. I didn't think much of this little mule at first but I come to love her. So it turnt out Mr. Oates done me a favor though he didn't suspicion it at the time.

I notice Miss Berk every time I went to her house would ask me, "Ed, do you need any help? If you do I'll hire you some."

"No'm."

One day Wilmer ask, "Is you got any grass in your crop?"

"A few bunches around."

Wilmer tell me, "You better get it out 'cause Miss Berk is comin out there next Thursday and Mr. Oates say your crop is et up with grass."

"It's not et up with grass but I'm goin to clean it out."

"Clean it out good."

Every day by sunup I had my mule workin. The cotton was high enough so I could plow as fast as I wanted. I sided over my crop good and get all the grass out of it.

I had done caught up everythin by Wednesday evenin. It was clean as a whistle. Thursday when Miss Berk come I was gone fishin. Next time I went to get my furnish money she told me, "You got the finest crop there is on highway 280." I was glad to hear that. I sure thanked Wilmer.

He helped me more than once. That fall Mr. Oates want me to move so he could put his son on my farm.

I goes to Miss Berk's house and she hear me talkin to Wilmer, which was what I want her to do. She come in the kitchen, "What's this I hear? As long as you treat me good and do like you been doin, that's your home."

She goes on out and Wilmer say real loud, "Well, Ed, you better go see Mr. Oates or you might have to be movin pretty soon." Then he whisper to me, "Let's see what she say."

Miss Berk pop back in the kitchen with her temper up. "You don't have to go see Mr. Oates or nobody else. That's my land and you can stay on it. Nobody is goin to move but Mr. Oates that I know anythin about."

She leave and Wilmer wink.

So that's how I got shut of Mr. Oates.

19 Some people around Abbeville claim Dr. Hart give animals Coca-Cola for medicine. But at Broxton rich white folks talk about him bein a high-class vetinary. I think he liked to doctor animals in Broxton 'cause it was in a wet county. He took to buyin too much wine and not enough food for his family and feed for his stock.

For the five hundred acre farm acrost the road from me, Dr. Hart paid fifty dollars a year rent to the government. It was mostly covered in Bermuda grass. In cool weather Dr. Hart pick some spots that wasn't covered as bad as others. Him and his boys, Abner, the married one, and Oakley, about twelve, plant a one-horse farm, scattered all over, a patch here and a patch there. But when it got hot they wouldn't work it.

They had three head of stock, one mule and two horses. Abner would take the mare and fasten her down in the thickest Bermuda grass and try to plow. A mule will strain and go, strain and go. But a horse will balk. Abner didn't want to work and he would take the mare back to the barn and claim she wouldn't work.

When the Harts first come I could set on my porch and tell just as good when somebody's animal had got sick and the doctor had got paid and brung home some food and a sack of mule feed. Smoke would come out the stove flue and little Oakley would go to plowin.

The corn was high enough to plow and the cotton hadn't been chopped.

One day both the Hart boys was at my house. We was settin under a tree in the cool.

Abner say, "Ed, you sure got some fine watermelon."

"You could have had some, too," Oakley told him, "if you'd a got out there and worked with me."

I didn't say nothin. Later I ask little Oakley, "When you gonna plant your cotton?" The mule was gettin thin. You can't work a mule on green grass.

"Ed, I ain't got nothin to eat, and I ain't goin to plow if I ain't got nothin to eat."

I figure a white man ought to be able to do better than me. He was free and had been. It ain't good to be free and got nothin to eat and nothin to wear, but the poorest white man want to think he's better than the richest colored man.

At that time near about all the whites was scared to eat with the colored, leastways if any other whites knowed about it. If I did some work at his house for some very poor man that didn't have nothin, he'd fix my food on a plate. Maybe he'd bring it out the kitchen in his hand. "Well, Ed, it wouldn't make no difference to me about your eatin in the kitchen but my wife don't like it."

Some of them would ask me in. Mr. Arnold had plenty cows, hogs, land, a seven- or eight-horse farm. When he got ready to eat he'd say, "Come on in, let's wash your hands, Ed, and eat dinner." His wife would put me at the cook table in the kitchen.

Mr. Thad Monroe was called the meanest man there. Him and his family had a big kitchen and they eat in it all the time. They would fix me a separate table and he would say, "Eat a plenty. Here your biscuits and syrup. Now if you want anythin we got over here, you just come get it."

But I'm the one fed Dr. Hart's family. About nine or ten o'clock most every mornin Dr. Hart's little red-headed girl Margie would come and tell my wife, "Willie Mae, I want to kill flies for my dinner."

We didn't have screens at my house. Margie was good at swattin flies and Lord knows we had plenty of them, so she was a big help to us. If you told her to do anythin, she'd run and do it. She was swift.

About eleven thirty her mother'd come and ask could she help for her dinner. My wife would fix a better dinner than for just us. She'd set Margie's mother to cleanin greens and we'd have cabbage and baked potatoes and milk and butter and, for dessert, blackberry pie or peach pie.

The Harts used to borrow a lot. They never would bring nothin back and never had nothin when you went to borrow from them. So me and my wife decide we wasn't goin to let them have nothin else. That day Oakley come. "Willie Mae," he told my wife, "Ma say send her some flour."

"I ain't got no flour."

Then he ask for meal and she give him the same answer. He smile at me. "Ed, what about a ripe watermelon?"

"Go to the patch and get it," I say.

My wife raise her voice, "I thought you wasn't goin to let them have nothin else."

Seem like I couldn't deny him. Anyway, I knowed if I deny the Harts borrowin they'd go to stealin. In the spring when my corn was in roastin ears they went in my garden at night to gather what they wanted to eat. In the fall they would turn their stock out in my corn in the evenin and get them back the next mornin. I got tired of them tearin down my corn.

I goes to Miss Berk and tell her I am goin to move.

"Don't move," she say. "Maybe they'll move."

I goes home and just as it get dusk-dark here come the horses and the mule. They had been shut up all day. I drive them right on in my barn. The next morning Oakley follow their tracks up to my place.

"Yeah," I tell him. "They out there in the barn. You been turnin them out on me at night."

He carries them on back home. As the Lord would have it, the people who sold them to the Harts come that day and take them back for lack of payment. You talk about a glad critter. I was one of them.

But I never was able to be mad at the Harts for long.

Many times I went with Dr. Hart to see after a sick animal. My secret fact was that from my earliest days I had wanted to be a doctor. I'd go to work on any animal I seen sick. I had a good nerve about doin things.

The reason I to take up helpin animals was my place got to be a dump yard for dyin creatures. Back in them days people would take a sick chicken and throw it off their property on to someone else's. That was one of the things I had to take.

When Dr. Hart first seed me operate a chicken sick from too many oats he laughed. "That ain't goin to work."

I knowed better. I have saved a many a one. When that chicken live Dr. Hart took to braggin on me. "Ed, you're just a natural born doctor."

When I first examine a chicken like that I found the craw to be packed full. The chicken couldn't get the oats up or down. I decide to operate. I pull all the feathers off the craw. I get me a sharp razor and when I cut I learnt a chicken has two skins to his craw, a thin inside skin and an outside skin. I wash the oats out the craw good with cold water. I seen the skins worked different so I sew them up separate. First I sew up the inside skin and greeze it with some meat drippins. Then I sew up the outside skin and rub it with a little fat. After I learnt myself to do that I hardly ever lost a chicken.

Many white people in my settlement if they had a cow or mule or hog sick would want me to come and help them. That way they'd save the doctor bill. If I seed I couldn't help, I'd advise, "Go get the vetinary."

In my helpin him feed his family and in doctorin animals together Dr. Hart and me was just like brothers. But not when other white folks was around. Dr. Hart was scared of them callin him a nigger lover.

I sent for him 'cause all of a sudden my cow took sick. I couldn't figure what ail her. She was way out with calf but not hardly due just yet. The evenin before when I had brought her to the barn she was healthy. The next mornin she was down and couldn't get up.

A friend come by. "I seed the oldest Hart boy ridin your cow last evenin." I figured he had broke my cow down so I would send for his daddy and they would get some money for doctorin her. When Dr. Hart come he said, "Yeah, I'll get her up in a little while. Go to the drugstore and get me one half pint of paregoric and some Epsom salts."

I knowed the druggist real good. He say, "That doctor ain't goin to give this paregoric to that cow. He goin to drink it."

"Naw, he ain't goin to drink it 'cause I'm goin to watch him."

My sister's three chillen was stayin with me and we was all seein after the cow. Dr. Hart say, "Go put on a kettle of water."

I want to watch him. I say to the oldest child, "Thelma, go put on a kettle of water."

The doctor ask, "Can you get me a cup?"

To the next oldest I say, "Jay, go get me a cup."

Then the doctor want a big spoon. I tell the youngest, "Get a big spoon."

Then he want something else. I had run out of chillen. I start for it and met Thelma bringin the kettle of water. "Watch him and don't let him drink that paregoric."

The doctor goes to the corn crib and she follow him. She call to me, "Uncle Ed, he drinkin it! He drinkin it!"

I run to the crib. I could tell he had swallowed somethin strong real quick and it was burnin him. "The druggist say you was goin to drink that."

He was pourin somethin in a glass. "It's in this glass," he claim.

I pick up the glass and what was in there didn't have no odor. I figured it was water. "I don't smell nothin in this glass."

"No, the cow's tension is killed the scent of it."

The cow died and when she did you could see the calf kickin her in the flanks.

"I could cut the cow open and take the calf out."

I was already vexed with Dr. Hart for drinkin my paregoric and I didn't think I could raise the calf without the cow. "No, I don't want the calf."

That wound me and the Harts up—whether or not Dr. Hart was ever paid in paregoric again I don't know.

20   After I give up my Model T, I waited about
four years and then got a Model A Ford single-seated coupe.
After a year I swap it for a 1930 Model A Ford sedan. It was
painted up good and looked pretty new but the tires wasn't no
account.

When me and my wife was settin down to breakfast about
six o'clock the next mornin here come Abner Hart. "You went
and bought this car?"

"I ain't paid for it. I got to work out the payments."

I had a little puppy on my porch. Just as hard as he could
he kick the puppy off the porch. Then he got in his car and lef
drivin like somethin after him.

Things was just beginnin to move forward, pullin up from
Hoover days. But I didn't have no money and couldn't seem to
get none. I got behind in my payments. The man that own the
car brought a man to drive it back. I tell him, "That note ain't
due today, it's due tomorrow."

"If you ain't got the money, what difference do it make if I
take it today or tomorrow?"

"I ain't got the money but I might could knock it up."

"We goin to Pineview to see about another car. See what can
you do."

I tell them to meet me at Miss Berk's house when they come
back.

Wilmer say Miss Berk at Mrs. Dunamore's. I set down and
talk to Wilmer. When I just had to I had been goin to Miss Berk
for two or three dollars. "You don't need that money. You tryin
to kill me like you did Mr. Addison."

Once when she was goin on I had got so tired of waitin for
her to get through I say, "Miss Berk, that's a pretty suit you got
on."

"I had it made from a suit of my dead brother's. I had to do that."

In place of smilin I just bust out laughin. Wilmer shake his head for me to stop. "Miss Berk," I say, "you know you's a rich lady."

"Money is very tight, Ed. How much do you want?"

After that I told Mr. Powell I had half a mind to move. He say, "What do you care about her fussin when she let you have the money right on?" That was the way to look at it, I reckon.

I leave Wilmer and goes huntin Miss Berk at Mrs. Dunnamore's. She had left there for Mrs. Erskine's. Mrs. Erskine say she just went home. I see her through the curtains in her livin room.

By then the men waitin to foreclose is settin out front waitin for me. I goes in and tell Miss Berk the situation. She didn't fuss at all. She walk to the window, pull back the lace curtains, and look at them men.

"Well, Ed, I thought I knew everyone. But I don't know them from Adam's housecat. I think instead of loanin you a payment I'll just pay the whole thing off. You got the note?"

"No'm."

"Go out there and tell them I never laid eyes on them before and I'm not payin till they bring me the note."

I was a little put out with them anyway so I tell them just how she said it. They ask me do I want to ride to Fitzgerald with them to get it. When they got out on the highway they really flew. I was scared. It was just between me and the Lord but I was askin Him for help.

Finally, the other man told the driver, "You might as well slow down. This boy ain't scared." He slow down and start drivin like folks. The owner had told me the bank had the note but he went straight to his house and got it.

Goin back, one of them say, "You mean that lady is goin to pay off this whole note?"

"That what she say."

"Boy, you better stay with her the rest of your days."

"You don't have to tell me."

One day Miss Berk told me, "Ed, I'm goin to sell out and go to Clayton, Georgia."

I didn't want her to go. It seem like I had a tender feelin for Mrs. Addison and Miss Berk. I just naturally run them some, but not as bad or as bold as some people would have. I'd ease around them.

"I got about thirty acres on the edge of Abbeville that I'm goin to help you get," Miss Berk told me.

I did not expect to be a landowner, but I jumped at the chance. All sorts of pictures come to my mind. I could see myself walkin around my land, settin in my house, callin all my folks to come and set at the table with me. I heard myself ringin the dinner bell and sayin, "Come and get it or I'll throw it away."

I didn't have no handkerchief so I kept wipin my eyes with my hands. Miss Berk left the library. When she come back she say, "Ed, if you sell this place, I want you to take the money and go to school."

"Yes'm."

"I'm goin to get you a right young mule. And I got a house in town we can move to your farm." I knowed the house. It was sealed and had sheet rock on it. "We can have it put near where Jim Powell live."

He the old colored man I planted peanuts for. "Well, I know he'd be proud to have me there close to him 'cause the Sanders been meddlin him."

"Go get that McDuffie boy up there around Polk City and tell him I want that land surveyed."

I got Mr. McDuffie and just as we was turnin off the highway here come Mr. Rufus Sanders. His property was next to that farm of Miss Berk's. When he seed Mr. McDuffie he hail him down, "What's for sale?"

The next time I seed Miss Berk she told me, "Ed, the Sanders don't want you to have that place."

My wife dreamed of seein the house Miss Berk was goin to move there for us burnin with us inside it.

Miss Berk was busy packin to leave. And she was tryin to

sell her property, a big hotel, a big buildin, a heap of houses, a law office she turned into a bus station, farms.

I goes to her house one Saturday mornin. "Miss Berk, I thank you for your gracious goodness in helpin me get that thirty acres. But I don't think I wants it. I wants the property where I'm at now." It was about one hundred and nine acres and three-quarters.

"I don't mind your havin it. But that place is right in the white folks' settlement and I'm afraid you might have a lot of trouble there."

One thing I didn't fancy about that place. The Sanders had to go through it to get to town.

And the Monroes, who lived on the next property, was known for bein a mean breed of white people. Whiskey or no whiskey, they would fight. They had a terrible killin of their own kin on their place a long time back and no colored would work for them.

Miss Berk say, "I'm afraid for you, Ed. You'll get along for a couple of years. But you're a good farmer. And if you take any money and go to fixin that place up, they'll want to borrow from you and they ain't goin to pay you back. Or they might burn you out. Wouldn't you rather have the place where Rogers is? I think you'd be better off 'cause they're colored people down where he at."

"No, Miss Berk, if you agree to me havin this place where I'm at now, I want it. Let come what will or what may."

When they heard the farm I was on was for sale, a heap of people come to look it over. Miss Berk say, "Well, everybody make me offers but nobody put no money down."

"Miss Berk, I'll give you one hundred dollars more than anybody else will."

"How much have you got?" she ask.

I reckoned the crop would bring about five hundred dollars. "I got two hundred and fifty dollars. If I go borrow money from the bank, they will get the interest. Why don't you loan me the money to buy it and you will get the interest. You can dispossess me if I fall down in my payments."

"All right. I think I'll do that." Our cotton was in the warehouse. "Go to town and sell the cotton and bring me the money."

When I got back from town, Minnie Lee carry me to the door of the bedroom where Miss Berk was countin money. She had tens and twenties and big bills coverin her bed, a plumb sheet of money.

"Here it is, Miss Berk." I give her the receipts and a little better than five hundred dollars in cash that our cotton had brung.

She helt it up, half hers and half mine. "We're goin to put this on your farm," she say. "Don't tell nobody I give you this money."

Until Mr. Sanders raise a fuss she was intendin to give me thirty-three acres. Instead, she give me half of the down payment on the place I was livin on, all her tools, two mules, hay rakes and hay mowers, and all the feed there at the time. "That goes with the farm." And she didn't charge me nare penny for furnishin me that year.

This was Saturday evenin. "Ed, Monday be down here about nine o'clock. We'll fix up the deeds." She wrote out a piece of paper that the property was sold to me for sixteen hundred dollars and I had made a payment of five hundred dollars and have five years to pay the balance. "This will take care of you if anythin happen to me. I'm old, Ed. Pay for this place as quick as you can. I'll never take it away from you, but if I die, you don't know what might happen."

"Miss Berk, you got good use of yourself."

"None of my people lasted much beyond seventy. I don't expect to be here much longer." Again she say, "Now don't say nothing about our deal, Ed."

"No'm." I figure she didn't want me to tell she had give me somethin 'cause I was a colored man and she was a white lady.

Monday mornin Lawyer Abraham fix up the deeds. The news got out that I was a landowner before the mornin had passed. If they had five hundred dollars, some of the colored say, they wouldn't give it for the whole world. I wanted me a home. They went right on. "You done played hell now. The white folks goin to have you in the woods every Saturday night."

Sun Fuller say, "You done bought that land now. You're a landowner. You can't go to town dressed up."

"Why?"

" 'Cause the white folks ain't goin to let you. They think you're gettin up with them. They ain't goin to let you wear no white shirts around town."

Well, it had me scared a little bit. But on Saturdays I'd put on my good clothes and go to town just like I had been. I didn't act no bigger or no littler than I had before. I stayed the same.

"You don't act like no big man."

"No, I ain't no big man. If I owned the whole world and all that was in it, I wouldn't act no different."

Some of my friends couldn't hardly change their clothes but I took up time with them. I didn't look over them and if they come to see me I treated them nice.

Mr. Thad Monroe was the main man I was sort of afraid of.

Mr. Monroe come over. "Ed, I hear that you bought this place."

"Yes, sir. I tried to buy it. But I don't know whether I'll ever pay for it."

"I want to ask you and I want you to tell me the truth: Did you buy it for yourself or did you buy it for someone else?" I suspicion he thought some white person could have got me to get it cheap for them. What had everybody puzzled was they didn't think I had the five hundred dollars. Which I didn't. And they all wanted to know where did I get it.

"Well, I got it."

"I'll tell you what," Mr. Monroe say, "as long as you act like you been actin and treat me like you been, anythin I got over there in the way of workin tools you can come at. You welcome to it. I want to help you."

When the Monroes poisoned they cotton the east wind

would blow the powder to my place and the flies and the dirt daubers there would go crazy. Everybody had gone to usin BHC. Arsenic and toxaphene wasn't strong enough to kill the boll weevils. The trouble with BHC was it would do more damage than you want it to. It has a stinkin scent and it don't make you feel too good, no time that you stay in it very long.

Mr. Thad Monroe come by. "Ed, you owe me fifty dollars."

"Why?"

"I poison my cotton. The wind blows and does yourn as much good as it does mine."

"Well," I say, "I do a lot of prayin and ask the Lord to help me."

I'll say one thing for the Monroes. If you was with them, they wouldn't let no other white people get at you. One day me and Mr. Monroe was settin on the curb in town. He had just got some batteries for his radio so he would be sure not to miss Amos and Andy. "Ed, what about us old country folks settin under electric lights with a radio before us?"

The rich folks in the country had been burnin lights. They had big batteries with a gasoline motor. But Mr. Thad got his lights and I got mine when the Georgia Power Company come down the highway with electricity.

"When was the first time you heard a radio, Ed?"

"That year I worked for the white Mr. Ed Brown his son Lester was friends with the son of Mr. J. M. Harvey. The Harvey boy had a radio. Lester would come home and tell us about how he heard a ball game in Atlanta. At first I didn't believe it."

I look up and seed Mr. Sanford comin down the street. When I bought an old Plymouth from him he did not overcharge me for it. He was carryin a feisty little puppy he had. When he come by us he say, "Look out, Ed, this dog love shit."

Mr. Monroe turn around and look at him and say, "Sanford, if that dog love shit he'd a been at you years ago.

Miss Berk ask me about carryin her to Clayton, Georgia, to her cousins. I had seed 'em in Abbeville and them cousins was an ugly set of people. Mrs. Addison had looked pretty nice when she got dressed up. But Miss Berk was short and stuffy fat. She was red-headed and a very settled lady so I reckon she must have dyed it.

When I was helpin Miss Berk pack to leave, old man Justin Summerville stood around there to her front door. He'd ring the bell and Miss Berk'd say, "I don't want to see him."

He would stand there on the porch for the longest. Finally he'd walk off. I ask, "Why don't you see what he want?"

"He want to marry. I'm not an old maid 'cause I couldn't have got married. I didn't want to marry. And I don't want to marry him."

"Why don't you go out there and tell him somethin so he can stop standin on the porch?"

"I ain't studyin him."

"Go out there, Miss Berk, and tell him now. I think that'd be right."

"I believe I will."

I hid where I could hear them.

"What do you want?" That was just the way she ask him.

"I want to marry you."

"What is you got to offer me?"

"I got myself."

"That would be a plenty. But I don't want to get married." He was an awful poor man and too old and he was talkin to a rich lady. "How come you wait till I'm fixin to leave here before you ask me?"

"I don't know. I just decided I want to marry."

"Then how come you don't go to church? I ain't never seen you in church. Or cleaned up."

"Yeah, but I could learn to."

She told him off pretty nice and he walk on off.

"He don't want to marry me, I don't think, Ed. I reckon he think I'll fall dead directly and he'd have my money."

I driv Miss Berk to Clayton. "You think being well off make life easy, Ed. It help some but you got to fight to live. We're dyin off."

After I leave Miss Berk you might say I felt lonesome. I wonder did she feel that way too. Shucks, she ain't thinkin on Ed Brown, I tell myself. I went on home, and she would come back and visit her friends there and she'd send for me and ask how was I gettin along.

21 I got behind one year 'cause I bought me an automobile. Cars and trucks was my problem now. They was too expensive. My wife wrote Miss Berk about the car. She wrote back can you pay your taxes? Always pay your taxes on time. And never mortgage your place for nothin.

But I did. I mortgage it two or three times. But I never let my taxes go. Sometimes I couldn't hardly hold all my promises together.

Me and my wife partition the house into three nice rooms. I put a porch on the back and we had a well and a nice fish pond. We had an outside toilet and a pump on the well.

An old seed house that Mr. Addison bought in Abbeville was our barn, a real nice one, and a lot bigger than most of the barns around town. It had shelter on the west side for the car and the tools and on the east side for the stock.

We was livin good. For Sunday breakfast at eight or nine o'clock we would have fried chicken with grits or rice, coffee, biscuits, syrup, butter and jelly. In the fall of the year sometimes we'd have rabbit for breakfast.

In my section both white and colored would put dishes of food all along the center of the table. Every man would fix his own place and take as much as he want. The clean silver, standin straight up in a glass, and the sugar and syrup stay in the center of the table all the time.

Dinner was the main meal of the day. There was no leftovers served at noontime. We'd have boiled meat, cooked cabbage greens or somethin else from the garden, peas or corn or collards, baked sweet potatoes, buttermilk or ice tea, your rathers on that. No farmers I ever knowed of liked lightbread. For dinner at noontime there was cornbread or maybe my wife would make eggbread, light and good. And she would make a quick cake if I had a neighbor to dinner, or a blackberry pie or a peach pie in the summer.

For supper we would scrap up anythin left over from dinner. If you didn't have no leftovers and had to cook somethin, it would be on the breakfast side, boiled or fried eggs, maybe a slice of fried shoulder meat, biscuits, buttermilk, coffee. My favorite way to fix supper was to take a bowl and crumble up cornbread and put either sweet milk or buttermilk on it.

A heap of times a man will tell you, "Well, I'm glad to see you doin so good," when all the time he hatin it. I paid for my farm and I got able to buy me a Dodge automobile nicer than anyone else in the settlement had.

Ardis come to my house one Saturday mornin and ask could he borrow ten dollars, he was goin to Fitzgerald to do a little tradin. I let him have the ten. My wife seed it and I seed it.

That mornin I had put a twenty dollar bill on the floor of my truck. Me and my wife was goin to town after dinner. When we got in the truck the twenty dollars wasn't there. For about two hours we look for that money.

We had give up when here come Ardis with ten dollars. "Brown, you give me a twenty dollar bill in place of a ten. I didn't use all that money 'cause I just ask you for ten."

Well, he had used twenty 'cause he had the ten I give him and ten out of the twenty besides.

"Ardis, I know that was a ten and you got that twenty out of my truck."

A few days after that—it was the latter part of April—I was layin off my peanut rows. I seed this big white smoke—it was my barn burnin. It was dry and had dry feed in it. I could see the wind was blowin the fire around and then back. The smoke had got big. I snatch my mule from the plow and away I went home. Some people was there before I got there. There wasn't no chance to put out the fire. My Dodge was burnt up with the barn.

Mr. Thad Monroe was standin around there. Away he went in his truck and in a few minutes he was back with ten bales of hay. Five bushels of corn and five bales of hay is what Mr. Marvin give me. Mr. Raymond Wolfe brought me a basket of corn and enough hay in his automobile for my mules' dinner.

"Hitch up your wagon and come on over there to Rochelle and I'll give you a load of hay and corn," Mr. Nobles told me.

"You can have all the hay I got if you'll clean it out," Mr. Terrell told me. He had changed from mules to a tractor.

The section boss, Mr. Cooper, had a little farm right on the edge of Abbeville. "Next time you go to town stop by and I'll give you some corn."

Central Shelley, a colored man, say he goin to divide what corn he had. He was workin stock and so was I. So I told him the people had give me more feed than I had lost in the barn.

All my close neighbors was white except Ardis. He live right up the road and he never did come to the fire at all. I been knowin him all his life. His mother, Rosie Griffen, had no husband. When she got pregnant with Ardis her folks turnt her outdoors. She come to my wife and me, and Ardis was born in my house.

The day after the fire my wife come runnin to the field where I was workin. "Somebody wrote on the gas tank," she say. It was one Mr. Addison had put there. I didn't use it. "Yeah, it say, 'Watch, Brown, it'll be your house next time.'"

I went with my wife and looked. I couldn't read it but I could see it all right. The ground around the tank was covered with Bermuda grass and there had been so much comin and goin about the fire it wasn't possible to track no one.

People would ask me, "How did your barn burn?"

"I reckon a rat got into a match and sot it afire." Some of them thought I was goin to leave there.

I call Mr. Raymond Wolfe "Mr. Raymond."

He said to me one time, "Ed, did you come by my house last night?"

"No."

"I knowed it wasn't you."

"How did you know it?"

" 'Cause you call me 'Mr. Raymond' and this fellow call me 'Mr. Wolfe.' "

That was what give me to think Ardis was the only man that call me "Brown."

I needed me a dry place to keep the feed for my stock. I sent for Ardis and we took the floor out of a tenant house on the place and made it into a barn.

While Ardis was helpin me I tell him, "I didn't have no insurance on my barn and no insurance on none of my feed and equipment. But I had eight hundred dollars insurance on my car and I got fifteen hundred dollars on the house. Let somebody burn it. They won't be doin nothin but makin me rich."

That house is still standin today.

The insurance man come out and look at the tank and he say, "Ed, the man who did this is low in statue and he ain't got no education worth nothin 'cause he didn't spell all of them words right."

I don't know how good Ardis can spell but he's sure low in statue. I got to thinkin through this. Every other man amongst my neighbors offer they service. He was home. And he call me "Brown." I just settle in my mind he done it.

The insurance company kept sendin men out there to get me to settle for my car. I had got me a policy for the cash value of the car, the eight hundred dollars that I paid for it. And I had paid two hundred dollars on it. So they owe me six hundred. They want me to settle for three hundred and fifty dollars.

"No, I been payin on that policy. Now I'm lookin for you to do what you say you was goin to."

They kept a comin. About nine o'clock one mornin, when the ninety days the company had to settle was just about up, here come another man. He set down on the swing on my front porch and went to rockin back and forth.

"Ed, I come to live with you."

"You did?"

"I'm goin to settle this before I leave here."

I had come out the field when I seed him stop.

"Just make yourself at home," I say. "I got to go back to the field."

At noon I come back and he was still there. He filled hisself up on dinner.

He say, "I'm not goin in front of no lawyer."

"Yeah? Why you don't want to go in front of no lawyer?"

I had talked with Lawyer Bartow in Abbeville. He knowed the situation.

"I'll go in front of a justice of the peace."

"O.K.," I told him, "let's go."

We got in his car and went to town. I had him to park near Lawyer Bartow's office. We got out of the car. He was walkin along, lookin at them papers. He knowed I couldn't read.

"Now I ain't settlin for less than six hundred dollars," I say.

"That's what I got these papers made out for."

He thought we was goin to the justice of the peace. I didn't stop walkin till I got in Lawyer Bartow's office.

Lawyer Bartow stuck out his hand. "How do you do, sir. I'm T. W. Bartow."

That man call his name. I didn't know it. I never seed him except that day. He went to sweatin. And he tore up them papers. "I got to fix some more papers." He wrote out some more.

Lawyer Bartow look at them and say, "This all right, Ed."

I sign them. That man lit out from there.

Lawyer Bartow took them torn-up papers out the trash basket. "Let's see what we got here." He pick up some pieces. "That joker had three hundred and fifty dollars written on this."

I tricked that fellow. But if I hadn't he would have tricked me. You have to study for yourself to get by.

You can get in a heap of tights farmin whether you're a share cropper or a landowner. The man furnishin you the money and seed and fertilizer and gas to make your crop has always been against you. He say what he want for his fertilizer. He say what he want for his cotton seed. About half of my farmin days I had to buy groceries from him. He say what he want for them.

For a long time I just look at it from the cropper's side. One time me and Dr. Durham was ridin along in his car. I was sayin how I thought most of the lawyers and doctors who own farms around Abbeville was real rich.

"They're sure not. Sometime they be layin woke all night long thinkin out where they're goin to get the money to pay you off Saturday. 'Cause they know if you don't get paid, you ain't goin to work the next week."

I found out that the truth.

A landowner will run up on other problems. Mr. Raymond Wolfe had some hands and they got to stealin my wife's okra and tomatoes. He say no they wasn't and sort of blowed up about it.

It happened as the Lord would have it that one day us both come down the road, me from Rochelle and Mr. Raymond from Abbeville. Them roads met at my place. Joe, Mr. Raymond's hand, was in my garden. So we all three met right there. Mr. Raymond say, "What you doin in the garden, Joe?"

"I was just lookin at Ed's stuff."

Well, I was lookin to see what Joe had. I notice a pile with some grass throwed over it, so I goes and kick off the grass and say, "Come get your 'matoes and okra, Joe."

"He can have it," I tell Mr. Raymond. "I just want you to know he takin it."

All the white folks went through with it. Before I had land if one of them there had a cane patch and I want a stalk of cane and he not there, well, I wouldn't ask him. I'd get it and go on about my business.

A neighbor will get to plowin. He'll draw up over your line if he can.

I advise a colored man not to buy a place back behind nobody. Buy a place out on the road. My place was on both sides of the highway. So I didn't have to go by nobody's house to come out to it. You don't want to have to go through somebody else's property and get picked on.

The AAA had come in. That was how I learnt to write my name. Back when I work for Miss Berk she had to sign for the subsidy and I had to sign for it. The thing was gettin sort of particular. I went to sign with a cross.

"No," she say. "You goin to write your name."

So she taken my hand and the pen and move it and made me write my name.

Comin back home, she was settin behind me in the car. She write my name on a piece of paper and hand it to me. "A nice young man like you that can't write your name. Here's your name on a piece of paper. You copy this until you learn how to write it."

I learnt and from that day to this I quit signin with a cross.

Now that I own land, I found that several of my white neighbors was puttin their cotton in the soil bank. They was gettin money without makin a crop. I wanted to do that.

I goes to the AAA and they had me to put five acres of my land in the soil bank and to plant ten acres in cotton. I had eighty dollars' worth of stock in the Cordele Production Company, so they let me borrow eight hundred dollars to make my crop.

My wife was sick, so I had big medical bills. My grandkids had to start school and didn't have no clothes. I sold the first bale of cotton I picked.

You can hold your loan man, he won't bother you, as long as you don't sell nothin. When he come to see you, you can say, "I ain't never got my peanuts thrashed or I ain't never sold my cotton."

The minute the Cordele Production Company got the news I had sold a bale of cotton they sent for me.

"You sold our cotton."

"I ain't sold your cotton. I sold mine."

That's a privilege you got when you have your own land or are farmin on standin rent.

"We furnished you in order to make a crop, so you could pay us."

"Why make a cotton crop when the government will give me as much as I can clear on it without all that work?"

They didn't want to wait for the subsidy check I was gettin for puttin my cotton in the soil bank and yet I had signed it over to them. They went to talkin about how I wasn't goin to get it.

"Yeah, I think the government is going to give it to me 'cause they promised it." I farmed before the government got in it and sold cotton for five cents a pound."

"What your folks doin if you ain't got a crop? Put your land in the soil bank and they ain't got no work to do."

"They got my peanuts to hoe. And they got plenty of other work to do."

I was wrong about it, I reckon. I had mortgaged them the crop. But I couldn't let my grandkids go to school naked.

One mornin me and Mr. Leslie Prince was both gettin our subsidy checks. Since that turrible year I worked for him I hadn't seed him.

He come up to me. "Ed, I'd like to have that twenty-four dollars. And I won't charge you no interest."

"I'd rather you'd charge interest." And I just kept a walkin.

By him takin everythin I made on that crop 'cept what I eat, he didn't allow me a livin chance. I didn't figure I owed him one cent and I never did pay him the twenty-four dollars.

Mr. Prince the worst I ever worked for and the Addisons and Miss Berk was the best, but I also got my share of white people that was not too good or too bad either. Just ordinary. Them I cheated, but not too bad, every once in a while when I got the chance, just like they did me.

Some would be straight. In them days you'd take balancers and peas—scales and weights some people call them—right to the field. My granddaughter, Emma Lou, was in high school and she would come with a notebook and a pencil. By my tellin her how much I was payin a hundredweight, she would figure how much I owe the pickers.

After I got my farm I hired many a white person as a day hand. If any of them said any slang word at me, I never stood and argued. I'd just walk on off. That's how I sometimes made it with the white folks. But most of them that worked for me treated me mighty nice.

There was a poor white family named Spies, right young people with four or five chillen. And I mean they was poor. They lived here, there, makin crops for various farmers. One year they lived in an old-fashioned, very rotton log house, one of the pioneer houses on Mr. Carter's place.

I had a big field of cotton, eleven or twelve acres that run up to Mr. Carter's line. My cotton open before his. Mr. Carter come over. "Ed, when you gonna start pickin cotton?"

"I don't know. I'll get me some sheets made up and then I'll start."

"The man work with me would like to help you."

"You reckon?"

"I imagine so if you'd ask him."

Some white people don't want to work for a colored person and some will. I think this fellow had sent Mr. Carter to ask me to let him pick. I ask Mr. Spies did he want to work.

"Yes, I'd be *glad* to help you. Your cotton just as good as anybody else's and your money just as good as anybody's."

I told him and his family just like I did the colored workin for me, "Do your work good if you don't do very much." If we was choppin cotton, I'd say, "Dig the grass up by the root. Don't just chop the top off 'cause come a rain, it'll take a bigger holt in the ground than it had the first time." Cotton I wanted picked clean. I told the Spies, "Well, you all hit it. I wish I had a bale now."

Later we was weighin up cotton. There was fifty-two cents

difference in the amount my granddaughter figured and what Mrs. Spies thought I owed her.

The lady point at me. "If my figures ain't right, I'm as black as Uncle Ed."

"Go set down and get this straight. I want to be fair," I say.

Mrs. Spies's husband took her figures. He set down on the cotton sheet. In a minute he looked at his wife, "Well, you're as black as Uncle Ed."

When she come back to Abbeville me and Miss Berk would talk about Rogers Hollis. Before it was over Miss Berk sure learnt Rogers. She lent him one hundred dollars to make a down payment on sixty acres of sorry land, way off, six or seven miles from town. With his mule and his crop as security he borrow one thousand dollars from the Cordele Production Company.

He buy two suits of clothes, leave Minnie Lee, and get him another lady, claimin wife, and goes to Florida on the train. Him and her just ride around spendin money. When the note is due he didn't have nothin 'cause he hadn't made no crop. The Cordele Production Company catch up with him and puts him in the Abbeville jail.

I carried him some candy and a Coca-Cola.

"Hey, how you, Ed?"

"Fine, how you?"

"Kickin, but not high. Floppin, but can't fly."

"Look like they kind of got you fenced in here. Is there anythin you want me to tell your wife?"

He say, "No. This ain't gonna be no handicap for me. All I want them to do is to give me a fine."

He was talkin like he own the bank. "Well," I say, "you all right then."

As I was leavin he say, "Look here, Ed, would you mind tellin Minnie Lee please would she get me out of here?"

I told her.

"I ain't studyin him," she say.

Mr. Snowden got Rogers out on bond, kept his case from comin up in court, and turnt him back to jail when the crop was gathered. This worked on the minds of the colored.

I was standin in Mrs. Ryan's store and heard her tellin people Miss Berk had passed.

I spoke out. "That was the best lady I ever knowed. You could sure put your foot on anythin she said and stand right on it. She never done wrong to nobody I knows of."

I had borrowed money from Mrs. Ryan. She was, maybe, as high as five feet. Her bank was in her bosom. She'd reach in there and bring out a big roll of money. "Now, Ed, this don't belong to the store. When you bring it back, bring it to me."

I walk out the store. I had lost a good friend in Miss Berk and I knowed it.

Mrs. Ryan follow me out. "Ed, I sure would feel proud if you was to say somethin like that about me after I'm gone."

"Yes'm."

Miss Berk left her niece, Miss Owens, land all over Wilcox County. She knowed me pretty good so she come out to my house. "I see you got your place paid for."

"Yes'm."

"Well, nobody can't bother you, can they?"

"No'm. I was lookin out for that. I thought Miss Berk might pass sometime and I wanted to have my place paid for."

Lawyer Tate seed me in town one day. "Ed, you ain't got a clear deed to your land. Thirty years back all of your place didn't belong together. There was about twenty-five acres of it was sold for taxes. Tell you what I'll do. For one hundred and twenty-five dollars I'll get you a clear deed."

Most all the white folks said it wasn't nothin but a fraud. Lawyer Bartow look in the courthouse and say Lawyer Tate right, so I paid him the one hundred and twenty-five dollars. I figure if Miss Berk had still had the property Lawyer Tate wouldn't have gone pokin his nose in her business and she wouldn't have had to pay.

22   There was mule dealers all around, in Abbe-ville, Pineview, two in Rochelle, two in Pitts, one in Cordele, and I don't know how many in Americus. Mr. Cecil Sapp sold mules on the west side of the street in Rochelle.

Scrub mules I call what he sold. Some of them was broken down like the ones the gypsies had. The day before they try to sell one they give him a salt block—a mule will eat a whole one in a night—and then in the mornin he'll drink enough water to fill out.

Some had worked on the road with the chain gang. You'd see one with fistula—that's a sore that won't heal—or a night eye—a hard spot on the inside of the leg. There'd be lame mules. Take a mule with cedar toes home and the hoof will always be breakin and crumblin off and shoes won't stay on. Some mules can go barefooted and some can't.

Mule dealin is just like tradin a car. Your mule ain't never worth nothin and the one the dealer got is. When they brought the animal up for folks to see, the auctioneer might call out, "Whose mule is this goin to be? She's gentle, straight, and sound in every way, about five years old, will work anywhere fast, a little weak in the eyes." You might find out the mule was one-eyed, won't work double, and won't work to a wagon.

Sometimes Mr. Sapp would have a mule he couldn't fool nobody with. Then he'd say, "We're sellin this mule at the end of the halter. Take her like you do your wife, for better or for worse."

If Mr. Sapp try to sell you a "bargain," a mule just a "little short in the wind," you'd know someone had overstrained him and that his wind was ruint. He would bellow and jerk for breath and his sides would just be heavin when he work.

The dealer has got the mule shut up in the stable, curried and brushed pretty and not nasty. He's in a clean place, well rested 'cause he standin in there and ain't got nothin to do. When they let him out in the back lot he's rarin to go and, man, he goin to cut a figure, wallowin and runnin around. He'll play. That what sell.

Say I'm the stable boy and you there ready to trade. It my job to make the mule the dealer is aimin for you to buy look lively.

I put a halter on him and punch him around a little bit. Some mules walk with they heads down. I keep my hand high on the halter to hold his chin up, so he'll sell.

And I keep him movin around. A mule make a better show from the back. I'm goin to carry him right where you is facin. Then I'll wheel him right around and turn his back end to you and let you look at that. The dealer is standin with you. He got a buggy whip and the mule know what that's for.

At the opposite end of Rochelle from Mr. Sapp was Mr. Giles Farr. He had first-class mules. Mostly he got them from Tennessee. One of the few auctions I knowed him to go to around our section was when a man convicted of murder was about due at the electric chair. The man was allowed to get out of prison to have this auction to pay his outstandin debts before he died.

It was in July 1948. Mr. Farr ask me did I want to go and I tell him I don't mind if I do. We went way off. I ain't never seed such a crowd. Later Mr. Farr tell me it was in the Atlanta *Journal,* that five thousand cars with seven thousand buyers was gathered on or around that farm that day.

Ninety head of cattle, many registered, machinery, and seventeen hundred acres of farmland was auctioned off. Mr. Farr didn't buy nothin. There wasn't many mules. Mostly we just walked around drinkin Coca-Colas.

The man going to the electric chair was fat and he was settin in a chair that turn around like they got in offices. He was fannin hisself and moppin his face and chewin tobacco. The juice was drippin out his mouth. People was walkin up to him and shakin his hand and tellin him good-by.

Mr. Farr didn't do that. He hadn't knowed him and he say he didn't think now was hardly the time to make his acquaintance.

I loved to look Mr. Farr's mules over at his stable. He'd have them in there in all colors: black—that was popular, especially with a white nose—and brown or red, bay—that's a light brown, almost cream—and blue, yes, blue. I don't think I ever seed a very sorry blue mule, one that was just plumb lazy. An iron gray mule has got gray hairs mixed with white, but he will turn gray all over when he gets older.

If you're buyin a mule, you want to look for good, clear eyes. Open a mule's mouth and see is he got deep cups in his teeth. Mr. Farr try not to buy any with blemishes, warts, cuts, bruises, or knots. That'll knock the price down.

Of course, a man not knowin mules can make his own trouble. One time when I was at Mr. Farr's stable a man from Macon come. "I want a fast mule and I don't give a damn how fast he is."

"I got just the one you're lookin for," Mr. Farr say.

Out come a mule I knowed well. It was one Ardis had worked and he was too fast to hitch to the cotton or corn planter and have the seed come out right. The man went on off with him.

A lot of people wantin a good work mule would try to get one with big bones and blocky wide. Some of them are just like a good settled person and will work along slow. But they ain't as fast as a long-bodied mule. They is high strung, easy excited, and will go till they give out or hurt theyselves.

Some mules are good at dodgin work—just like some people. If you hitch a lazy one double, he'll walk along behind with his traces slack and let the other mule carry the whole load most of the time. You can hit him and he'll jump up then drop right back. You got to make him go on and do some work.

Some of 'em you can just talk to. "Gee," he gone to the right. "Ha," he fall right back to the left. "Come up," he move on off and you can feel him movin just like you can your automobile when you put gas in it.

They'll mind you just as good, and some of them a whole lot better, than kids will.

Do you like breakfast? A mule the same way. Some people take them right to the field without feedin them but before I eat my breakfast I would go to the barn and give my mule five ears of corn and a thin block of hay or a bundle of fodder.

It's a heap easier to keep a mule well than to get him up after he go down. I fed them hay and dried corn and sorghum cane. Mr. Farr really liked my havin any mule he had. "Whoo!" he'd say, "you really takes care of them."

You have to look out for a chile. And you have to look out for stock, most especially a fast mule. One of the biggest things to watch is don't let your mule get too hot. When he go to pantin heavy, stop and let him rest. And if he do get too hot don't let him drink water. If he do that a mule will almost always die right then.

It gets hot before the cotton is laid by, rangin from 80° to 100°. On a big farm more than likely they would ring the bell at eleven o'clock or eleven thirty. If you was up with your plowin in June and July, you hardly ever plow right up to twelve noon. That's hot on the stock and hot on you too. You'd go to the house and stay there till about two thirty or three o'clock. Then you come back out and plow long as you could see.

I've knowed mules to make twenty crops and then look good. Some folks don't have no feelin for stock. Let them stand out in the weather and don't half feed them and they won't last long.

I always listened to my mule. There's a difference between a mule whimperin and brayin. Some of them, not all, you can hear holler out on the highway. And a jackass you could hear him holler from here across town when he bray.

You hear him whimper heeeeeeeeeee. He askin you for some

feed or he's thirsty for water. He'll let you know he want somethin and you go in the barn and give it to him.

He got plenty of sense. He just can't talk.

If he's workin and it come noon, he's ready to knock off from work. He'll go toward the house fast but not so fast away from it.

I bought one mule from Mr. Farr that I couldn't get hitched to nothin. The first Sunday mornin I had him about seven men was to my house tryin to help me. We blindfolded him and had another mule to hitch with him but he went to backin and side twistin.

Men was on the ground with lines holdin him and there was two in the wagon but he just runned away into the open field.

I went to see Mr. Farr. "I can't do nothin with him with half the people in the settlement helpin me. And I got to make a crop. He ain't broke."

"He supposed to be."

"Well, he ain't."

So I trade for a black mule with a white mouth. He had come from up north and he wasn't used to our climate. Old sand flies and horseflies bit him and he broke out. Both sides of his neck had raw places.

Miss Lacey saw me walkin to town. "Ed, why you walkin your mule?"

"This mule got sores. I'm takin him back to Mr. Farr."

When I come back by, Miss Lacey call, "You carryin your mule home?"

"Yes'm, he wouldn't take him back. But he did cut the price some."

Miss Lacey come out to the road and walk around the mule. "Ed, this is a right nice mule." She look at the sores. "Get you some creolin. Now don't make it strong. That will upset him. Just make it sort of weak and bathe that place with it and see won't that do it."

Why I not to think of that, I don't know. The mule shook all over. His harness was just a wavin. "Look at that," Miss

Lacey say. "The weather will change in twenty-four hours when
a mule does that."

That evenin there come a big rain.

Back when I worked for Mr. Leslie Prince, I didn't like owin
him for whatever time his chillen spent helpin me. But I didn't
mind swappin time with Stuart Prince, Mr. Prince's stepson.

He was a fellow didn't want nobody to outwork him. But
once he got behind in his crop. He ask how about me and him
plowin his cotton. I helped him out.

After a while I want Stuart to pay my time back. He come
at sunup with his brown mule—snuff colored, I'd say—short
and dumpy, a mare. I was plowin a long black mule.

A mule is just like a person. When he first gets out in the
mornin he's stiff. He got to get limbered up, stretched out, and
ready to go to work.

My mule had long legs and was fast walkin. When Stuart
Prince wasn't lookin I'd just barely tech him with my lines.
About eight or nine o'clock his ears went to floppin backwards
and farwards. Backwards and farwards. He was free. He had got
the spirit. Him and me was ready to go. When I come to the end
of a row I'd reach way up close to his head and pull him around
right fast.

With a smart mule like I was workin you pull him around
once or twice, and after that he'll turn in a hurry so you won't
snatch at the line again. From end to end we went. It take a good
mule and a good man to go like that.

At that time I didn't have no limit on what I could do. Not
any. Stuart was goin to keep up with me like I kept up with him.
A little before night Stuart ask me, "Ed, would you plow the
task row?" That's land you've turned to cut the speed of the
water down and make it drain out of the field without cuttin a
ditch.

I went up to it. He kept on goin on the flat land. He went
that row. Then he come back and pull off his shoes. Me and him
had worked together a lot. He never had did that before. I was

makin like I wasn't payin him no 'tention. We goes to the end
of another row and back.

"Ed, I got to tell you the truth. I'm just give out. I'll help
you some more another day."

"Man, I'm just gettin ready to go."

I was as give out as he was. He gets on his mule and goes
to the house. I take mine to the other end of the field and lay
down there until sundown. When I drug up I couldn't hardly
take the mule back home.

There was that time when I wasn't workin for Mr. Leslie
Prince nomore but I hadn't moved yet. I heard a big commo-
tion, so I looked out the window and see Mr. Stuart Prince
beatin some mules. He was tryin to drag some logs to the road
to carry them to the sawmill. The mules got up pretty close to
the house and stalled.

"Come up!" he say. One'd fly back and the other'd go farwards. Mr. Stuart was beatin and cussin. He wasn't exactly
mean, but he didn't understand the human nature of mules. If
you treat one nice, he'll love you and lay his head on your
shoulder and want you to pet him.

A mule will shun a mean person. I have seen mules' mouths
cut and sore from snatchin at them with the line. People got to
give account of that, I believe. This mornin Mr. Stuart had got
to fightin the mules and doggin them and they had got to fightin
too.

I set there lookin out of the window. Finally I decide I
believe I'll go help him out. "Don't bother them," I say. "Just
let 'em quiet down." He got out the way and turnt it over to me.
Them mules knowed me. I had been there almost twelve
months.

I caught one of them by his ear. I whisper to him that I want
him to move his load, to get on out of there. Then I turnt that
one a loose and went around and told the other one about the
same thing. Next I pick up the lines and just loud enough for
them to hear I holler, "Let's move." Off they went.

23 Old Man Carl Henry Carter knowed I couldn't read and he'd set and read the Bible to me. A heap of times I have listened to people read, and I would get more understandin than the one readin.

Esau was the first born. Them chillen was twins and they got to scufflin while they ma was carryin them and causin her so much worriation that she put it to the Lord: "How come do I live?"

And the Lord told her she had two nations fightin in there.

Mr. Carter claim Jacob was due to be the first born but scrappin like that they got moved around and Esau come first. He was hairy.

The way it looked to me, Jacob stole his brother's birthright But Mr. Carter say he was just gettin back in his rightful place.

Sometimes after Mr. Carter'd read me about Jacob and Esau, I'd see him peerin at my arms. He'd look to see if I was hairy like Esau.

"I'm not hairy much."

"You's more hairy than I is."

That set me to puttin him alongside of Jacob. Him and Jacob was both tricky. Mr. Carter was a great man to get the ups on you.

Him and me traded my mules and all my farmin equipment and my seven hundred and fifty dollars for his one-row tractor. The deal call for me to pay him the seven hundred and fifty dollars in two notes, one due this year, and one the next.

Most likely he'd come over to my house on Sunday mornin. He'd done been to church on Saturday 'cause he is a Primitive Baptist and believe what is to be will be and that the other churches isn't hardly fit to go in.

Mr. Carter say not everybody can go to Heaven. But the

man that is goin is already chosen. Your goodness will most
likely keep you out of trouble here, but it will not get you into
Heaven if you was not chosen from the beginnin. A sinner who
is already saved can go right on to Heaven when he die. But the
Lord'll punish him here for everythin he done sinful in his life.

I am a Missionary Baptist. Accordin to my belief, if you sin
and don't pray and ask the Lord to forgive you for your sins,
you will go to hell. But we sure believe that a man can be a sinner
and then change and be a Christian and go to Heaven.

The mules I swapped for Mr. Carter's tractor was the finest
Mr. Giles Farr could sell. When you seen one at the livery stable
that look good to you, Mr. Farr'd open a gate and cut that mule
out in a back lot for you to see. If one didn't have much git-up,
I didn't want him. That was an old man's mule.

My mules weighed fourteen hundred pounds apiece or
mighty near to it. I bought them real young and pulled they
baby teeth right there in my barn. Emma was black with a
white mouth. I had just about broke Minnie—she was the
iron gray one—when I made the deal with old man Carter.
You couldn't drive them too good out on the highway yet.
And I'm goin to tell you the truth. I could not keep up with
them workin anymore, which was what put me in mind of a
tractor.

The one-row John Deere tractor Mr. Carter swapped me
had very little equipment with it. And time I got it and rid
around on it a day or two, just tryin it out, the axle broke. I goes
and tell Mr. Carter about it.

He say, "Well, those things will happen."

I had to go all the way to Albany, Georgia, to get me another
axle. The man at the John Deere place thought I worked for Mr.
Carter and I learnt Mr. Carter had been there and knowed about
the axle all the time, but he had not spoke of it to me.

The year I had the tractor I didn't understand it. It work out
good if you're plantin early to put down plenty of seed. But I
planted too much. I had the gauge on my planter wide open. I
used right smart of fertilizer so the cotton got high and give the
boll weevil too much shade.

I didn't make a good crop that year and Mr. Carter didn't either.

About three days before the note was due I ask would it be all right to pay what I could and to pay interest on the balance. Both of the banks would have been glad of the deal. I owned land and I usually made a pretty fair crop and they knowed it.

I show Mr. Carter the papers when I sold my cotton and peanuts and he knowed exactly how much my crop had brought. I thought he could see I wasn't tryin to fool him, and me and him could get together.

Mr. Carter say, "Well, I can't pay my debts either. Pay whatever you can."

So I goes home and don't think no more about it.

The mornin the note was due Mr. Carter driv up in my yard before I could get out of bed.

In place of sayin "Good mornin," he say, "Ed, what you gwine do about that note?"

I knowed right then somethin was up. "What you want me to do?"

"Well, if you ain't got the money, I guess I just as well get the sheriff. I reckon I'll get me a warrant and foreclose on you and take the tractor back."

I spoke right up then. "Warrant for what? I don't see no need of the law. Give me one hour and I'll have it back in your yard."

After a while he say, "Bring it on over."

I could have kept him from takin it back by goin to the bank and borrowin money. But the tractor wasn't worth my mules and tools. And it wasn't worth the repairs.

I didn't have nothin in this world to farm with when that tractor left. But my land was still there. Mr. Dewey Morrow was the first found out about it. He had to pass backwards and farwards by Mr. Carter's house to get to town, and he seed the tractor there so he come over.

"Ed, I see your tractor and all your equipment is back over to old man Carter's."

"Yes, sir, he want it back, so I let him have it."

"What you gwine do?"

I reckon I'll try to get me some more mules and mule equipment."

He had knowed me all my life. He study a minute. "I got all my mule equipment, and I've done stopped farmin with mules. I'm gwine home and pile up all my mule equipment and you can come look at it."

I goes over there and he ask, "What will you give me for them tools?"

"Well, they yours. You know what you want for them and I wouldn't want to price the other fellow's stuff."

"Is it worth twenty-five dollars to you?"

"Yes-ss, *sir.*" Them tools would cost me two hundred dollars to buy.

Then I say, "What you gonna charge me for the mule?" I knowed he had one blind mule.

"That is a present." He give me this mule.

So a week from the day Mr. Carter throwed me a dirty deal I had me a blind mule and plenty of tools to farm with. I borrow me some money from the Cordele Production Company for seeds and other run bills and I was back in business farmin.

It's right aggravatin to work a blind mule if you been used to workin one can see. You can put a mule that can see right in the middle of the row and he'll stay there and walk straight along pretty good. But a blind mule is just like a blind person. He walk wavy like and will get out of the middle of your row onto your crop.

If you hook them double, a seein mule will guide a blind one. Then you won't have to see after him no more than for stumps and holes. Don't let him walk into nothin like that 'cause that'll upset him pretty bad.

This blind mule come in mighty handy for breakin up my land that year and I made a good crop: nine bales of cotton and four tons of peanuts. And on my farm I had me some corn, syrup, sweet potatoes, chickens, two sows with they litters, and a cow.

I didn't go down. I was still there. And so was Mr. Carter.

He told Mr. Davis Barfield that he was goin to get his finger around my land. Everybody knowed he was raring to wind me up fast.

One mornin we come out on the highway at the same time. Mr. Carter had got him a Dodge pickup truck. He run by me and wave his hand for me to come on. I pull out after him in my old blue pickup truck my grandson had tore up. We was going up Fuller Hill. It's pretty steep and just as we got to the top he slam his brakes on and stop.

He thought sure I was going to hit him. I couldn't see over the hill, and if somebody had been comin up that hill, I would have had an accident. But I just took the chance. In place of runnin into him, I cut around him there on the hill and kept right on goin to town. I never did say a word to him about it.

Now he had the tractor back, he want to get me in debt so he could take my land. It broke me up from racin. I never did that again.

Mr. Davis say, "Ed, if I was you, I wouldn't go in no credit deals with Mr. Carter, nothin I couldn't pay him off right now. Don't fool with him."

I was scared of him but his land join mine and I had come to know he was so crooked I was afraid not to make like I was foolin with him.

When a thing is not right it will sure burden your mind. And I don't think Mr. Carter felt we had a righteous deal. He kept askin me what I thought about it.

I would say, "Oh, that's just business," so as not to fall out with him.

It seem like he got lonesome. The colored people and the white people sort of beared around him. He was there at his house by hisself 'cept for his wife. So I couldn't fall out with him and yet I didn't exactly love him.

Mr. Carter kept claimin he was already saved. Some things happen that put me in mind of how the Lord was punishin him here.

The first thing to aggravate Mr. Carter was that my mules

never did like him. The first year he had them, as long as I had the tractor, I would help him catch them whenever they got out and come back home. I could walk right up to them 'cause they liked me. After he took the tractor back I quit helpin him catch them. I reckon you could say I had got a little angry with him.

One afternoon I had company. The mules come and I just pretend I didn't even see them skirtin around the house. "Why didn't you head off my mules?" Mr. Carter say when he come runnin. I slam the door and set down with my company.

The mules lit out again. They went down to Mr. Arnold Steele's pasture where he had two hundred acres of land and jump over the fence and away they went. I was glad. I wanted them to give Mr. Carter trouble.

Then sure enough trouble caught up with him. He decide he want to build a fish pond. He had my mules and that same tractor he took back from me. I goes over to help him.

He had one fellow with a Yellow Gal saw for cuttin out the big trees, mostly black gum and a few sweet gums and a few pines.

I was tendin two jobs. Me and Willie Gene Newman, another colored gentleman, was usin a cross saw cuttin out shrubberies and small trees. And I was hookin logs and Mr. Carter was draggin them out. I would saw until he come with the tractor and then I'd go put a chain around a log and Mr. Carter'd pull it.

The last log I chain was not too big but the trouble was Mr. Carter was goin uphill and the log got hung behind a stump. In place of goin, the tractor just stood straight up and fall back on Mr. Carter.

He call, "Ed, Ed," mighty pitiful. I got him out and laid him on the ground, run to his house, and get his wife, his pickup truck, and a sofa. Me and Willie Gene lay him on the sofa and put it in the truck. And away I goes to town with Mr. Carter, me and his wife.

He was broke up. He told me he had jumped some. By him being old, he didn't get far enough off. The seat hit him below the belt. When we got to town the doctor look at him and say there wasn't no use of unloadin him, he couldn't do him no good on account of his pellis bone was broke and we'd have to carry him to the hospital in Hawkinsville. His wife got the ambulance and taken him there.

So he stayed off about a week. When he come back and his wife had to go off, she'd want me to come over there and stay until she come back. He couldn't get out of bed. And he couldn't always do his business in a pan he brung home from the hospital. He had to wear a napkin just like a baby. I'd see after him the best I know how.

After he got better he'd come over and say, "Let's go to town and get a Coca-Cola." He had some sort of spittin disease. He kept somethin runnin in his throat all the time. It got so I could hardly tend to my business. "Let's go to the doctor." He would want me to drive him there.

By bein sick, Mr. Carter had some expenses. A loan company write him his credit good. Mr. Carter write them back and ask how good is it.

He say, "Ed, don't you need some money?"

"Yeah, I need some."

"I got a man comin next week. I'm goin to borrow me some. Then I'm goin to send him over to your house so you can borrow you some."

The man come from the loan company. Mr. Carter can read the Bible but he is not educated for readin loan company writins. Before he knowed it, he borrowed about three thousand dollars on his timber. It wasn't no great big sawmill timber but it was real pulpwood stuff.

He come to know before he sign that he was payin the loan company 10 per cent, which was a mighty steep interest. But he did not know until after he sign that he had agreed to pay the man that drawed up the papers some extra.

The man come right to my house. "They tell me you want some money," he say.

"Yeah, I'd like to have some money. How much do the company charge?"

"Ten per cent."

Then I say, "And how much do you get for fillin out the papers? A high-educated fellow like you ain't workin for nothin."

He puff up and say, "Six per cent."

So I know it's 16 per cent. I say, "Well, you sure ain't gonna let me have none, 'cause I don't want it like that."

"That's the way we let it out," he say, "and we let plenty of folks have it."

To meet the payments Mr. Carter had to let go his only cow, then his hogs, and then that field of timber. He told me, "Ed, you was wise by not borrowin that money. It was the worstest money ever I borrow in my life. They is about cleaned me out. That fellow wasn't nothin but a crook."

Mr. Carter couldn't handle my mules no more. After another year he swap them to a fellow from down around Owensboro for a pair of little biddy mules. They didn't never get out, as I knows of, and if they did, they didn't come over to my house. He hadn't long had them before one of them died.

I guess Mr. Carter's faith suits him. But it sure look like the Lord is chastisin him here.

24 Mr. Dwight Ring, clerk of the court in Abbeville, write me a letter to come see him. This had me scared
'cause I didn't know what he want. I goes down there.

"Ed, they've gone to makin federal juries out of the colored.
They want a colored fellow out of every county. I figure you're
our very best person."

"I can't read and write."

"That don't make no difference," Mr. Ring say. "You go
ahead. Look for a white-haired man, name of White. Give him
this letter. When the clerk of the court call the roll you say
'present.' "

I brought the letter on home and my wife look at it. She tried
to talk me out of goin. You have to be sick or have a mighty
good excuse to get out from it.

"It's a high honor to be on a federal jury," one of the deacons
in my church tell me.

Another say, "Well, I don't know as I'd fool with that."

One say he thought they should have picked someone with
an education from the colored.

I say, "I'm goin and see how I come out."

Me and my wife got up before day, got in the pickup truck,
and went to Americus. I had to be there and upstairs in the post
office buildin by nine o'clock. I was clean. I was dressed nice in
a brown, double-breasted suit and tan and white slippers.

Mr. Ring had told me to look for the American flag. "That
the post office." When we got inside I ask for the federal jury
room. My wife wouldn't ride the elevator. I had to walk upstairs
with her.

She read the signs and when I went in the jury room I seed
an old gentleman with white hair. "Mr. Ring sent me."

"You Ed?"

"Yes, sir."

"Go over there and set down."

I was half scared to death 'cause I hadn't never been on no court. They had a roll call. Then they tell me and several white men they wasn't goin to need us. We was loose until after lunch. I went down on the street and walk around and goes to the colored cafeteria. After lunch they turnt me loose for the rest of the day.

I stay around there for a while and I learnt a heap just settin there listenin. Some colored was there for stillin and sellin liquor. The judge was a low, stout fellow and he wore a black robe like a preacher.

He would ask the accused, "Don't you want a lawyer? Don't you want to defend yourself?"

One was cryin—pure cryin—tears. "No, sir, I'm guilty."

"You ought to have cried before you fired up your still," the judge said.

I was with the judge on that.

The white and the colored drank out of the same fountain. You'd put your finger on a button and the water would jump up. I never tried to get ahead of nobody there. A lawyer walk up to the fountain. I stood back and he drank. "Thank you," he say. Then I drank.

One call me "Mr. Brown." It put a different feelin on me.

In our county courthouse in Abbeville, they would make the colored sit on a bench right in front of the judge. Many times I've heard him say, John, Oscar, Henry, stand up. I got you accused of stealin, stillin, fightin. I give you six months (or twelve months, or whatever come in his mind) hard labor on the chain gang.

Once I heard the judge tell a tall, brown-skinned fellow, "Robert, stand up. I give you six months or fifty dollars."

Robert say, "Thank you."

The judge open his mouth wide but didn't say nothin. He studied Robert for a minute. Then he rap on his desk. "Twelve months or one hundred dollars."

Ardis was there. His idea was, "The judge thought by Robert sayin 'thank you' he was takin his sentence too easy."

None of the colored thought there was justice. It was more of a crime to steal somethin minor from a white man—it didn't matter how hungry you was—than to murder another colored man. The white people didn't care much about that then.

If you was a good worker, you wouldn't have to stay in jail long. A white man could come and say, "Turn my nigger out of jail. He ought to be plowin. My mule's standin still."

That was the kind of court I was used to before I come to the federal jury.

They put me on a moonshine case. You talk about scared. I was scared I wasn't goin to tally up to what they want me to do.

A white bootlegger was charged with sellin unlegal whiskey. The law didn't catch the man with the liquor. It was acrost the road from his house in an old house that nobody live in. The law was you had to catch a fellow with the whiskey on him or on his property.

He did not plead guilty. And he had a good lawyer who got up and put a lid on everythin the solicitor was tryin to do to chain-gang the accused.

When we went into the jury room the rest of them went over to a table and set down. I walk over to the window. One of the men say, "Looks like we're mixed up here."

"Yeah," another tell him, "they use 'em now on the federal jury."

I was chewin gum. I knowed they was talkin about me.

I went over to the table and took my place. We went to discussin the case. Most everybody had spoke. The foreman ask me, "How do you vote?"

"They didn't catch the liquor on him," I say. "The liquor wasn't on his property. I don't think they can lay it on him. 'Cause the law is he's got to have it in his possession. So I reckon there's nothin to do but clear him."

The man that mentioned mixin say, "That nigger work his mouth like a damn billy goat."

Nobody seem to pay him that much attention. I have learnt that if a white man can't get other white men to join in tormentin you, he'll soon stop.

After I answer the foreman's question he ask the rest of them, "Do you all agree with that?"

There was a white fellow from Pitts, Georgia. He was dirty and his clothes was nasty. He look like he could have come right out of the field. "Well, yeah," he say. "That's about the way of it."

So we all voted to clear him.

The judge told us, "You all gentlemen may think you ain't competent but you is. You may not think you accomplished nothin by bein here but you did."

After that I seed the bootlegger outside on the street and he wave and smile at me. He didn't know me by person, just by face.

There is a lot of money to be made in the federal jury business. They payed you twenty dollars a day then as long as they kept you, whether you work or not. That's one reason they didn't want the colored, I think. Up till then that was the most money I ever made in one day.

I went to Americus to the federal jury two or three times before any whites in Abbeville knowed it except Mr. Ring. But once when I went the deputy sheriff from Abbeville had a case up there. "Ed, what you doing here? I didn't know you was here."

"I'm on the federal jury."

"No!"

When I got back to Abbeville everybody had got in the wind of it. I didn't care about the colored knowin. But I wasn't so sure about the whites. They don't want you to get ahead of them.

"The Honorable Ed Brown," Mr. Carter say to me. "The Honorable Ed Brown."

25 If you ever been around someone who has lost they mind once and got well, you can tell if a change is comin again.

My wife was afraid the lights in the house was goin to electrocute her. One day I had to go off and when I come back she was pilin up wood around the light wire post. I got her not to burn the wood and my grandson put the wood back in the woodpile.

She taken eighty dollars of the money I got from the Cordele Production Company to make my next crop with and she hid it somewhere. "I don't know where it is," she claim, and I never did find it. Next she broadcast pennies up and down the road just like she was plantin somethin.

She got jealouser and jealouser. When you're farmin you got to get who you can to gather stuff from the field. She'd come and run my cotton pickers off.

The most notice Willie Mae give of her mind bein bad was when she broke up Mrs. Monroe's funeral procession. Mrs. Monroe was a white lady live near us and she had owed my wife some money for a long time. She was not goin to pay, she say, but she would give my wife some clothes. They was wore out and not fit to wear.

When Willie Mae seed Mrs. Monroe's funeral comin down the highway, she tie some wires together to start the truck—we didn't have no key for it—and got out on the highway drivin on the wrong side. Once the hearse come close to her she turnt around and tailed it by bustin right into the procession.

I was workin in the field and seed what happened. Seem like I was just waitin to hear a crash. I run down on the highway and wave down a white man. "Give me a ride, please sir. I'm tryin to head off my wife. She ain't in her mind."

"Oh," he said. "I met her down the road apiece." He let me out near where she was and I talk her down and brung her on home.

"I ain't goin to wear Miss Monroe's old raggedty clothes," she say.

To put my wife back in the hospital I needed my sister-in-law Maureen to help me. I didn't like her too much. She was meddlesome in my business. Her husband, John B. Lockwood, was afraid of her. He turpentine and he wasn't even allowed to cash his check. "Let me tell you, I wouldn't be under that petticoat government," I'd say. But he'd do it 'cause if he didn't go her way, there'd be a fight.

It was a cool day when I went to they house, and John was setting outside in the sun right up in the chimney corner shuckin corn. I set down with him and start shuckin. He say, "You sure don't have to help."

"What you gonna do with them shucks?"

"I reckon I'll burn 'em."

"How about givin 'em to me for my cows?"

He look towards the house and whisper, "Maureen don't want you to have them."

Maureen come to the door and I ask her about sendin Willie Mae back to the hospital.

"If you go to Heaven, I don't want to go," she say and slam the door.

I hadn't been caught stealin or meddlin nobody. I hadn't been out fightin to amount to nothin or in front of the law. That family treated me just like I was an old throwed-away person.

I just leave it to they brains. They wasn't exactly right. One time Doll went to New Jersey. She lost her mind and was put in the hospital there. They sent her chile to me and my wife.

My wife had an aunt at Hawkinsville that went in the mental hospital.

I had done what I could to keep Vine from bein a bootlegger and when I couldn't do that I give him money to pay his fines.

He claimed I was dumb to work. But everybody knowed he wasn't smart enough to be a bootlegger. He commenced to have apoleptic fits and died.

The last time I seed my wife's other brother, Emmett, he was layin in the mental hospital at Pineview cryin and cryin.

But if one of them got in trouble, they'd flock right to you.

I went to see the clerk of the court to find out was there any way for me to put my wife back in the hospital without her sisters signin papers.

"Ed, it's been two weeks since they come here and sign them papers." For meanness they was tellin me they wasn't goin to sign them.

The next day me and the sheriff took her to the hospital.

The doctor there say, "Your wife is old and I don't know whether she comin back this time."

I had already told myself that if I got her in this time, I was not goin to get her out. When someone is sick you'll wonder how will you stand it till they leave for the hospital. Yet and still when they leave you'll be lonesome.

I got sick. Dr. Durham ask, "Ed, you got any money?"

"No, sir. I ain't got much money."

"Why don't you go downtown and be with the other folks? You gonna stay out here and get in the same shape your wife is." He been knowin me a long time. "Take you a little money and see what you can do to enjoy yourself."

I start takin that medicine. When I got home late from the café there wouldn't be nobody to fuss or argue. I could get up the next mornin and hire anybody I want to help me on my farm.

Now I'm goin to tell you the truth. I sort of liked it—goin when I got ready. I had me a piece of car. I thought I was havin a big time. Nobody to say nothin.

I had married when I was sixteen years old. A heap of men just go out every Saturday night spendin they wife's money on this lady, that lady. But I hadn't been doin that. No liquor to amount to nothin, clothes just passable so I could go, no nothin anytime until I provide for my family for the comin week.

Now I got to goin amongst the ladies a little.

If you got a loved one in the hospital, everybody will point they finger right at you. Willie B. Taylor had a wife in the state hospital. So far she had stayed there fifteen years and he never had been to see her and he didn't let his chillen go see their ma.

But every time he would meet me he would ask how was my wife gettin along.

"She doin pretty good."

Most especially if I'd be with a lady he'd ask, "How your wife?"

"She ain't no better."

I was sort of bruisin around town. One time I seed him comin. I had taken my wife away from the hospital and taken care of her as good as I could. I loved my family. But Willie B. Taylor was vexin me. He come at me. "How your wife?"

"She doin pretty good. How is your wife gettin along to the hospital?"

Me and him have had many conversations since and he never did ask about my wife again.

I'd get dressed up and go to the hospital to see my wife, but not regular like I did when she was there the first time.

When I ask her how was things there she would whisper and look around like someone was goin to jump on her. She tell me she had been whupped. I talk to another lady about it and she say the one who did the whuppin is a right young girl. She was born at the hospital when her mother was a patient there.

When we was talkin this stout young lady come into the room. She is carryin a switch and she got bad sores on her face.

"That's her," my wife say.

"Yeah, that her," the other lady say.

I run up to her. "I hear you been whuppin my wife."

"Boy, you better tell your wife to mind," she say and kept a walkin.

"Look a here. She ain't used to mindin."

She went into a room and close the door.

I didn't like that. I got an appointment with the doctor. "Every time I come here my wife has fallen off some. She's gettin down to where she look poor."

He look at her chart. "She won't eat."

Now I was whisperin and lookin around. "If they whups her, she can't eat."

A funny look come over his face. He set there lookin at me a minute, then he get up and walk off. He didn't come back and after a while I lef.

When I went to town Flu Helen Stokes, a little dark woman, not black, would look at me and smile. I would look for her, and if she wasn't there, I'd wonder where was she. One day she come up to me. "Plant a dollar on me."

"I got to plant a dollar where it'll grow."

I was studyin out a way to see her. I knowed she live with her auntie.

"If you come to town," Flu Helen say, "you see my auntie go to work about eight o'clock. Then you come to the house."

Early the next mornin I go downtown and set on the lazy bench in front of the cafeteria. After a while here come Flu's auntie. I just eased on down to Flu's. That's the way the thing got started.

She was smart about workin and she knowed everybody in town. After I got my crop in and up she'd help me get a big bunch of hands and we'd go in the field choppin cotton.

Flu was an awful drunk sometimes. But she call herself religious and went to the Elizabeth Church in Abbeville. The members there was tryin to raise money. Sometimes they would give a box supper. I found out Flu would get other people to bid on her box. I'd have to put out to top them.

Flu was a big talker and she would jump right up and go. A heap of people call her Tiger. "Let's go where the crowd at," she'd say. For a while we had a big time.

We went to the carnival show to swing and ride, and three times I carried Flu to see a movie called *King Kong*. That was the first time I seed New York—in *King Kong*. I didn't believe it could look that way.

One Sunday afternoon I went to get Flu. Time we got in the car she said, "I'm pregnant."

"Pregnant! No!" That was somethin I hadn't figured on. I study on it awhile. "All right. I'm goin to help you. But if I find out this baby ain't mine, I'm goin to throw you in the Chatahoochee River."

Flu had about come due when my wife write me to please come to the hospital. I went. The doctor want to see me and I tell him, "My wife look like she gettin along fine."

"She want to go home. Do you want to take a chance on takin her home?"

Drivin home from the hospital, my wife got to talkin and laughin. "I reckon you got a girl friend."

"I don't have none but you."

I didn't know what to do. That's the truth if I ever told it. I stop goin to Flu's. I didn't hardly think I should go there now that my wife was home. But not goin there was worryin me too. About two weeks after I got my wife back Flu had twins.

Those babies was what pull the cover off me so bad. You've heard tell of people on a pedastool where they ain't goin to do nothin. Folks say I don't think he would do that. When them babies come, it was just like they jumped in the newspapers. In a little place don't nothin happen but everybody know about it. They tell from one to the other about it.

My wife's sister Maureen come to me and say, "I hear you got chillen in town while Mae was in the hospital. Look like you could have went with a lady that kept your name better."

"I could have, but I didn't."

My wife's sisters was afraid I was goin to marry again and

not take my wife back. Her and her sisters was wantin me to put her name on the deed to my land.

"Oh, all right," I tell them.

My wife went with me to the courthouse. When the clerk of the court heard what we want he ask me to step in another room with him.

"Ed, I ain't tendin your business. But with the fix your wife is in I advise you to leave this like it is."

I eased out of there. "You don't want Sister to have nothin," Maureen say.

"Yes, I want her to have somethin, but I want to have my land where I can boss it. I ain't goin to give it away. I ain't that crazy yet."

That was the best thing I ever done.

After the kids was born I stayed off from Flu's about two weeks. She sent this one and that one to me. Honest Johnson, a real good friend of mine and a deacon, tell me, "Flu say come. Course, it's with you whether you want to go or not."

"You seen the kids? You think they mine?"

"They do look just like you."

I make up my mind and goes there and see 'em.

My wife don't know nothin about this. The third Sunday of the month we went to the service at the Kramer Baptist Church. Some of them long-winded talking women tell her everythin they had seed me do and a lot they hadn't.

Her and her sisters say them chillen weren't none of mine. "Them ain't yo' chillen."

Doggin me. Breakfast, dinner and supper. My wife didn't give me nare minute's rest till I owned up to them chillen. "I won't never do it again if you'll forgive me."

My stomach is the weakest part about me. I had ulcers. "You must be rich," Dr. Durham say. "I've knowed rich people to have them. And I've knowed newspaper folks trying to get the news to have them."

"I'm rich with trouble."

It got so milk was about my only food, the only thing that didn't hurt my ulcers. I think what really got to my stomach was

that my daughter raised about as much sand about them babies
as my wife did.

I ask my wife for forgiveness but she wouldn't forgive me.
So I say to myself I don't care if you don't. She would tell me
what this one and that one say. Flu was drunk here, Flu was
drunk there, Flu did this, Flu did that.

Gus Turner was a man a whole lot older than me. "You ain't
done no big sin. The first men was after God's own heart. They
had a bunch of wives and concubines. I wish the kids was mine.
I wouldn't care what nobody say. If I was you, I'd enjoy them
and do all I could for them."

Flu got pregnant again. "What you tryin to do? Tie me up
tighter?" I didn't like it.

I never thought of leavin there until Ernest Johnson—Honest Johnson we all called him—left. One fellow like him in a
little settlement can hold it up pretty good. He was a deacon at
the Kramer Church and dutiful about comin and knowed how
to conduct the business for it. He didn't have no education but
he had good sense. He was a good friend I could go and talk my
troubles out with.

One time me and him was layin on some cotton, waitin to
get it ginned. He had took the chillen of his wife's sister when
she died. I was askin him about sendin them to school.

"I done sent my own to school. That enough."

"They'll come up like you and me. They won't have no
education.

"Well, I can't help that."

The night he went off many people from Kramer Church
come to the bus station to tell him good-by. Some cried when
he left and so did he. After that it seem like I just got in a fidget
and wanted to go.

Honest Johnson left 'cause he couldn't get nowhere. Nobody
in Abbeville ever seed him again but we heard he was firin a
boiler, got too hot, took a cold drink, and died. He didn't get
what he wanted in Abbeville or where he went. That happened
to many who left the south.

Sometimes if they couldn't make it, they chillen would get a little schoolin and things would be some better for them. I've knowed that to happen.

A lot of people left the south like Shorty did. He borrowed twenty dollars from Mr. West and promise to farm with him the next year. That's what he promise Mr. Thad Monroe when he borrow thirty dollars from him. Professor Bell lent him twenty dollars. My son-in-law carried him to the red light at Cordele. From there nobody knowed where he went.

Mr. Monroe tell me, "If I ever see Shorty again, he's goin to give me my money back. And until I get my money back I'll be glad to pay anyone a dollar a pound for his meat."

Things in Abbeville and Wilcox County kept shrinkin down. People you seen on the street today would be gone tomorrow. When I was a boy and a young man there would be so many people in town you couldn't hardly walk either of the streets on Saturday. All the stores had yards with hitchin posts for mules and horses.

A heap of the colored left after World War I. They kept goin, whites too. The next big movin was when the colored left goin to the Florida boom. Then durin the panic they left for Detroit and New York and other places.

Mules went out of style. And with them most of the jobs a man could put his back into. As long as farmin was done by man and mule power, a man with no education could get by. But after machinery come in, it got to where you needed more education than good sense.

I always felt sorry I didn't get no education. When I lived in Kramer, a lot of people in that little settlement couldn't read and write. So we decided we'd get up a night school if we could get the teacher. She agreed and she was a good teacher and knowed how to get you started out. I liked her and I liked to go to our night school.

The daughter of the family the teacher boarded with would

come with the teacher. But I think she was a little afraid to walk home just with this girl. One evenin the teacher ask who would walk a piece of the way with them.

I told her, yeah, I was glad to walk with her. My wife's brother decide he'd go. We walked on talkin and laughin clear to the man's house where the teacher boarded. When we got there we just turnt around and walked on back.

The man put it out that I was tryin to court the teacher and Vine, his daughter. As the Lord is my secret judge I didn't say nothin out of the way to the teacher about courtin. But at that time if a school teacher sort of looked like she liked a man, they'd fire her.

The teacher sent us word for nobody not to come back account of what had happened. So that ended that.

Without no education to speak of and without jobs you didn't need an education for, most of the colored was out of luck. One reason it got hard to find a job was the people who run Abbeville was narrow-hearted about lettin some businesses move there. Nothin with a union nowhere about it was fit to come.

The merchants in a town can build it up or they can kill it. So they kilt Abbeville. They would try to cheat your eyes out. For a while the farmers tried to cheat them. But the merchants was able to beat them at that.

There was lots of ways to cheat. Mr. Ace Harper would buy corn and peanuts for some big firm. He was they agent in town. When he first moved there he would buy all the peanuts around there—thousands of tons—'cause he was the nearest market we had.

The government man who went around and check all the scales in the warehouses was supposed to keep them balanced. Instead of that, he fix them for Mr. Harper, so he could short weight everybody.

I was in Mr. Harper's office when the government man come in. "What about my peanuts?"

Mr. Harper say, "Well, there's some back there. Go and get you some of them."

"I don't want just no few peanuts. I'm talkin about a lot of peanuts for the work I been doin for you."

I knowed that man was suppose to be workin for the government. And after that I learnt Mr. Harper's own brother was takin his peanuts to Rochelle.

You don't pay nothin for grindin corn at the mill. Instead they take some of your corn for a toll. They make meal of that and sell it to the stores.

Mr. Rufus Sanders own the mill. One time I hear him say to the colored guy workin there, "Did you toll that corn, boy?"

"Yes, sir."

"Toll it again. If he's rich, he won't miss it. If he's poor, keep him poor."

When they knowed they was beat, the farmers stopped tradin in Abbeville and went to other places around there. So it got to where Abbeville had no mill, no gin, no market.

Willie Mae quit workin and didn't want nobody else workin with me. Not even the grandchillen. I should give her some of the money I borrowed from the Cordele Production Company to make the crop, she say. And she kept doggin me for tradin our mules to Mr. Carter for his no-good tractor. I had had two more tractors since then but she didn't think about that.

She threaten to take off my turpentine cups and put them in the fish pond.

The evenin she come at me with a pitchfork I didn't forget her mind was bad. I ducked off from her. But I promise myself, if the Lord be my helper and I can get through gatherin this crop, I'm goin to rent this land and leave here.

One Saturday mornin my wife tie all my clothes in a sheet and put them out in the pasture.

I got my peanuts and cotton out the field and sold that. I told the high sheriff, "I'm fixin to leave here. I don't want you to think I'm runnin away. My land stands good for what I owe."

The sheriff understood. He had carried my wife to the asylum twice. I figured before I hurt her or got hurt, it was best to check out.

I tell Flu, "I'm goin to leave here. Do you want to go?"

"No. I ain't goin to leave my bat nest for nobody."

She didn't want to get married 'cause the money she was drawin from her dead husband—he was a soldier—would be cut off. I couldn't blame her much.

Sometimes a man will court an extra woman. That's how I got in with Darlene.

For years she cooked for Mr. Dempsey Claude Lander and his wife. He would drink a right smart of whiskey, then he'd go to the table and get mad and take the dishes and throw them out the window. Or he'd go to the icebox and pull everythin out of there and throw it on the floor.

His wife would go to cryin. "I'll get it up," she'd tell Darlene.

"That's all right," Darlene would say. "I'll get it up."

She got tired of that and quit them and got a job doin domestic work with some people in Atlanta who was goin to New York. The people want to hire a couple. Darlene ask did I want to go.

I was half sick with my ulcers and workin only about three days a week. Ridin a tractor kept me jolted up. I was rarin to go.

The last day I was at home I dressed a hog that had been run over and put it in the freezer for my wife.

When I come through the colored section in town on my way to get the bus to Atlanta, Mrs. Nat Walker was out sweepin her yard. I have swept yards all of my life mostly with gallberry brooms that we got down in the swamp. I have always fought grass tryin to keep it out of my crop. If you sweep away from the house all the time, you'll put your house in a gulley the water will stand in. You have to sometimes sweep back to the house.

It was such as that I knowed. Now so I could leave Abbeville, I was hirin out to work inside a house. I always figured there wasn't nothin to it. Now I ask myself can I do it.

I wonder would I go to New York with Darlene and the couple she work for. Two or three times I had seen *King Kong* brought from his country where he was a god or a king to New York, where he went to the top of the Empire State Buildin. The people got airplanes and machine guns. He was shot many times. Finally he fall off the building.

When I got on the bus I had a job waitin for me in Atlanta and four one dollar bills in my pocket. I thought, if I had to, I could walk back.